Description Of "the Brinkley Collection" Of Antique Japanese, Chinese And Korean Porcelain, Pottery And Faience...

Frank Brinkley, Edward Greey

Nabu Public Domain Reprints:

You are holding a reproduction of an original work published before 1923 that is in the public domain in the United States of America, and possibly other countries. You may freely copy and distribute this work as no entity (individual or corporate) has a copyright on the body of the work. This book may contain prior copyright references, and library stamps (as most of these works were scanned from library copies). These have been scanned and retained as part of the historical artifact.

This book may have occasional imperfections such as missing or blurred pages, poor pictures, errant marks, etc. that were either part of the original artifact, or were introduced by the scanning process. We believe this work is culturally important, and despite the imperfections, have elected to bring it back into print as part of our continuing commitment to the preservation of printed works worldwide. We appreciate your understanding of the imperfections in the preservation process, and hope you enjoy this valuable book.

INTRODUCTION.

Immediately after the abolition of the Feudal system in Japan (A. D. 1871), when the Ex-Daimio were pensioned and retired into private life, the art treasures that had, during centuries, been collected by them or bestowed, for gallant services, upon the *samurai* of their clans, and by the latter valued equally with their honor, were suddenly "thrown upon the market," not, as many foreigners imagined, "from a desire to put away childish things and adopt Western civilization," but because a radical change in social conditions had brought many a man who had lived in affluence, face to face with want, and the princely establishments of the Feudal chiefs in the Eastern capital (Tôkyô) were broken up at the fall of the Shogunate, and the art treasures they contained ruthlessly dispersed.

Among the first to understand this state of affairs was Captain F. Brinkley, who, in addition to a refined and cultivated taste and a profound knowledge of the keramic treasures of Europe, held a position in the Imperial service that enabled him to satisfy his desire to possess the finest examples of the art productions of the Japanese and to study the subject with native connoisseurs. He soon discovered that the beautiful specimens of porcelain, pottery and faience, then considered by foreigners "so common," had cost their late owners fabulous sums, and had been collected by persons of perfect taste and judgment, who also placed great value upon the keramics of China and Korea. He knew that "the golden shower" would soon cease, and availing himself of it to the full, secured the magnificent examples of color, glaze, form and decoration described in the following pages.

Captain Brinkley, like all of us who have written or lectured upon Japanese keramics, derived important information from the works of the late Ninagawa Noritane, whose friendship he enjoyed for many years and from whom he purchased a great number of superb pieces of pottery and porcelain. Simultaneously with forming his collection he began to secure material for a "History of Japanese Keramics," which is the only work upon the subject worthy of a connoisseur's consideration. The greater portion of his collection was obtained during the first five years after the political change, but later on he never hesitated to discard inferior specimens for superior, or to pay the increased value of the fine objects he desired, his great aim being to procure gems with which to illustrate his book. The Brinkley collection may, therefore, be most truly described as unique, for, during the Feudal times, when each piece formed part of the treasures of some lord or gentleman, no power less than that of a Shogun could have brought them together even for a few hours, and now it would be utterly impossible to secure in Japan even a small number of such specimens.

Upon purchasing this collection, I printed the description of each piece, furnished me by Captain F. Brinkley. Since then I have received from him the text and drawings of his admirable "History of Japanese Keramics," and a revised copy of the Catalogue. I have, therefore, before offering the collection for sale in my gallery, decided to reprint the Catalogue and, under each heading, to give excerpts from his forthcoming book.

While the numbers, &c., of the specimens, remain as first published, the dates, given to the various pieces, have been carefully revised by Captain Brinkley, who, in many instances, has only been able to approximate them, it being difficult to decide the exact time of their manufacture.

This famous collection contains superb examples of antique Chinese and Korean porcelain, pottery, and faience, and a most unique and complete historical collection of Japanese keramics, each example bearing the *cachet* of Captain Brinkley, our highest authority upon the subject. Its dispersion, while regretted by admirers of art, will afford connoisseurs, collectors and the trustees of museums, a rare opportunity to acquire exquisite specimens of ancient Oriental ware.

Those who may be desirous of purchasing any portion of the collection, can obtain information as to price, &c., at my Art Gallery.

EDWARD GREEY.

20 EAST 17TH STREET.
    NEW YORK.
December, 1885.

"In the days when Britons were living on acorns and dressing themselves in skins, the Japanese wore exquisite silks, used vessels of faience or lacquer, had attained a remarkable degree of artistic skill, and surrounded themselves with evidences of the highest refinement."

JAPANESE PORCELAIN AND POTTERY.

BLUE AND WHITE PORCELAIN.
BY SHONZUI GORODAYU.

"In 1510 a potter named Gorodayu Go-shonzui made his way to China in search of information, as Shirozayemon had done nearly three hundred years before. He was a native of the province of Ise, but of the incidents of his career prior to this journey, which was destined to make him famous, no authentic record is preserved. He made his way, first to Foochow, and afterwards to Kin-te-chang, where a course of five years' instruction and practice rendered him familiar with the methods of the Chinese potters, though he failed to acquire the process of enamel-painting over the glaze.

"On his return to Japan, he made no attempt to manufacture anything but porcelain decorated with blue under the glaze. Neither was this, strictly speaking, a Japanese ware. Shonzui had brought both the clay, the glaze, and the colouring material from China. None of these were then known to exist in Japan, nor were they discovered for a considerable period afterwards. When, therefore, the imported supply failed, the manufacture naturally came to an end. Shonzui settled at Arita, in Hizen.

"The clay he had brought from China cannot have lasted many years, and he had no opportunity of replenishing it. While it did last, however, he turned out very beautiful specimens. They were not distinguished by delicacy. Solidity rather than delicacy was required in pieces such as those to the production of which Shonzui devoted himself—tea-jars, water-vessels, censers, and cups for the *mat-cha*. The great beauties of his ware were in the glaze and the colour. The former was of extreme softness and lustre, while the latter was a blue of the finest tone and brilliancy. It is still a moot question whether the credit of inventing the celebrated "Hawthorn pattern," belongs to Shonzui. Many specimens of his ware now extant exhibit a variety of that design, and we may confidently assert that his decorations display the first unmistakable traces of the "Natural Style" as applied to Japanese keramics."—From BRINKLEY's *History of Japanese Keramics*.

No. 1.—Tea-Jar (*Cha-tsubo*). Height, 2¾ in. Diameter, 2 in.
> Design, diapers with circular medallions containing archaic figures. (From the collection of Ninagawa Noritane.)

No. 2.—Plate. Diameter, 5½ in. Design, Bamboos and Birds.

No. 3.—Pair of Wine Bottles, gourd-shaped, octagonal in section. Height, 8¾ in.
> Decorated in eight vertical strips of various Diapers, each alternate strip containing figures and floral subjects in white on a rich blue ground.

No. 4.—Cylindrical Tube for holding Tea-mixer. Height, 4 in. Diameter, 1½ in. Decorated in Horizontal bands of diapers and letters.

No. 5.—Wine Bottle, cylindrical, with narrow neck. Height, 9 in. Diameter, 3 in.
> Body divided by horizontal lines into four bands of decoration; lowest vine pattern in white on blue ground; the second, diapers and flowers; the third, landscapes; and the fourth diapers. The neck decorated inside with spiral bands of blue. This piece is a Chinese imitation of Shonzui's ware. Date, 1700.

No. 6.—Tea Jar, Stoneware. Height, 17 in. Diameter of body, 11 in.
> Decorated with blue under the glaze. Round the middle of the body the Seven Sages are grouped, with accessories, after a Chinese painting. Round the bottom is a band in which the sacred Horses are depicted, and round the top, a band of conventional flowers and clouds. The lid and neck are in repousće bronze of very rich workmanship. This piece is by Goroshichi, a pupil of Gorodayu Shonzui. Its date is therefore 1540. It illustrates the transition period of Japanese porcelain manufacture, when the clay brought from China was exhausted and porcelain earth had not yet been discovered in Japan.

IMARI OR HIZEN PORCELAIN,

DECORATED WITH ENAMELS OVER THE GLAZE.

"Shonzui, on his return from China, about 1516, settled at the village of Arita, in Hizeñ. The nearest port to Arita is Imari, a name familiar to all collectors as the common appellation of Japanese porcelain. After having exhausted the materials which he had brought with him from the Po-yang Lake he failed to discover any suitable substitutes in Japan. Yet, strange to say, in the spur of the very hill which rose over the village where he lived inexhaustible quantities of the much-desired clay were waiting to be used. His pupils and successors, Gorohachi and Goroshichi, were not more fortunate than himself, and the factory at Arita had almost lost the reputation acquired from his productions when there arrived there one of the Korean experts whom the Japanese generals had brought back from Korea by the *Taiko's* orders. This man's name was Risampei. Tradition says that in his own country he had acquired some reputation as a manufacturer of the celebrated "Ivory-white," and the story sounds probable, for, had Risampei, like the great majority of Korean Keramists, been familiar with the manufacture of pottery and faience only, it is most unlikely that he would have struck out an altogether novel line of his art in Japan. He had worked at Arita during two, or perhaps three, years, when, about 1599, he discovered on the slopes of Idzumiyama (the Mountain of Springs) a white substance that promised to supply the long felt want. Resembling rather stone than clay, this *shiro-tsuchi* (white-clay), as the Japanese commonly called it, had to be broken and pulverized in mills before the potter could employ it. It was in fact the *Petuntsu*, or feldspathic rock, of Chinese Keramists."

"Risampei's ware was known, in the days of it first manufacture, as *Kinko-yaki*, Kinko being the name of his native place in Korea. We have said that the decoration of his pieces was limited to designs in blue under the glaze. The fact is that neither Risampei, nor any other among the large number of Korean potters brought to Japan by the *Taiko's* generals, could impart to their conquerors a knowledge of the methods of applying vitrifiable enamels over the glaze. It may be that the development of this process was checked by a comparatively trifling lack of information. The Japanese, already wonderfully skilful in other branches of technichal art, would scarcely have been at a loss how to imitate the enamelled porcelain of China, had they not failed to perceive that, the vitrification of the enamels being effected at a much lower temperature than the baking of the *pâte*, the two operations must be conducted separately. But the Koreans ; were they too ignorant of this? Among the numerous specimens of old Korean faience and porcelain preserved in Japanese collections, the writer has seen only one (No 780 in this catalogue) decorated with coloured enamels over the glaze. This piece is attributed to the end of the sixteenth or beginning of the seventeenth century. It is certainly not less than two hundred and fifty years old. But, if its existence seems to show that the manner of using vitrifiable enamels was not wholly unknown to the Korean Keramists of Risampei's era, its unique character shows, equally, that such a process was altogether exceptional. Certainly Risampei was not acquainted with the secret, nor did the potters of Arita learn it until nearly half a century after the Korean discovery of porcelain clay on Mount Idzumi. The honor of making this great addition to the Keramic resources of his country is attributed to Higashidori Tokuzayemon. Like Toshiro and Shonzui, he seems to have contemplated a visit to China. With this view, it is said, he went from Arita to Nagasaki, in 1648, and there awaited an opportunity to carry out his purpose. Nagasaki was then a flourishing town of some six or seven and twenty thousand inhabitants. The Portuguese had been expelled thence eleven years before, but the Dutch had been settled in Deshima since 1641, and from seven to ten of their ships entered the harbor annually. It was with the Chinese junks, however, that Tokuzayemon had to do. These, too, came from time to time ; and it so happened that Tokuzayemon, explaining the purpose of his journey to a junk-master, learned from the latter the very few points which were needed for commencing the new style of decoration. He hastened back to Arita and made his first essay with tolerable success. His chief idea appears to have been to imitate the Chinese enamelled wares of the Wan-lieh period (1573-1619). But, as the attractions of these depended chiefly upon the brilliancy of their enamels, and as the Japanese potters lacked experience principally in this very branch of their art, no very satisfactory results were achieved. Among Tokuzayemon's fellow workmen, however, was one, Kakiyemon, who fortunately became impatient of imitative limits, and conceived the idea of adopting a line in better accord with his country's art instincts. The result was a chaste and very beautiful porcelain. Instead of loading his pieces with diapers and archaiac designs in red and green enamels, Kakiyemon made the decorations a subordinate feature, and sought, by careful painting and refined conceptions, to compensate what was lost in richness of effect. No one who has examined pieces decorated in the style which he inaugurated will deny that his success was remarkable. The *pâte* of his ware was fine and pure, giving a clear, bell-like ring when struck. The milk-white glaze, charmingly soft, yet not lacking in brilliancy, formed a ground harmonizing excellently with the ornamentation, which was simple almost to severity. The enamels were clear and rich in tone, but of few colours; a lustreless red, a grass-green, and a lilac-blue constituting nearly the whole palette. Of the decorative subjects, floral medallions were, perhaps, most common, but the dragon, the *Howo* (phænix), the bamboo, the plum, the pine, birds fluttering about a sheaf of corn, and various kinds of diapers, were constantly depicted. The characteristics of this ware are not only the sparseness of the decoration but also its distribution: instead of being spread over the surface, the designs are confined to a few places, the object apparently being to surround each little picture with as ample a margin as possible."—From BRINKLEY'S *History of Japanese Keramics.*

No. 7.—Trumpet-shaped Flower Vase. Height, 23 in. Diameter of neck, 10½ in.

> Decorated in blue under the glaze and colours over it. The centre is occupied by an irregularly shaped band surrounded by black lines, within which are flowers and conventional lions (*shishi*) in blue, red, green, and gold. Above this band the spaces are filled with diapers and floral designs. The upper rim is surrounded by a fillet of silver with rich filagree work stretching into the interior of the vase to preserve it from injury. Date, 1650.

No. 8.—Jar. Height, 18 in. Diameter of body, 10 in.

> Very rich and unique decoration. Round the neck a black band with a scroll design of vines and peonies in red, green, and gold. Below this a broad band of green with raised design of plum, pine, and bamboo branches, and medallions containing landscapes. On the body, three large medallions with landscape, peonies, and chrysanthemums. The spaces between the medallions are covered with rich black glaze and floral scrolls in red, green, and gold. Round the bottom a green band with conventional designs in red. Date, 1690.

No. 9.—Large Jar. Height, 31 in. Diameter of body, 16½ in.

> Richly decorated. The body occupied by floral design with trees and *Howo*, the spaces above and below, by irregular medallions and scroll patterns in gold on a blue ground. The top has been slightly cracked and is covered with a bronze cap pierced in a floral design. Date, 1680.

No. 10.—Large Jar. Height, 32 in. Diameter of body, 16 in. Octagonal in section.

> Decorated in panels with floral subjects and birds, the intervals filled with bold scrolls in deep blue relieved by peonies in red, white, and gold, and by diamond-shaped medallions, from which are suspended cords and tassels in gold. Date of body, 1760. Lid of modern manufacture and Kiyoto clay.

No. 11.—Deep Plate. Diameter, 19 in.

> The centre occupied by a landscape surrounded by a blue band with leaf scroll. The rim a rich broad scroll of vine leaves and children at play. Date, 1780.

No. 12.—Large Bowl. Diameter, 17 in. Depth, 5½ in.
>Covered inside and outside with a profusion of cherry blossoms, among which are houses and clouds. Date, 1700.

No. 13.—Large Plate. Diameter, 23½ in.
>Centre occupied by a basket of flowers with two circular medallions, containing landscapes and figure subjects. The rest of the surface divided by radiating lines into seven spaces, alternately decorated with floral medallions on a deep blue ground, and cherry trees, houses, and horses. Date, 1770. Mark, two peony branches.

No. 14.—Shallow Dish, with circular bottom and sixteen-faced edge. Diameter, 13¾ in. Depth, 3 in.
>Outer and inner sides covered with diapers and medallions; bottom, with figure and floral subject. Mark, *Fukki Choshun* (wealth, honour, long life, and happiness). Date, 1740.

No. 15.—Shallow Dish, with circular bottom and twelve-faced edge. Diameter, 10½ in. Depth, 3 in.
>Central decoration, a conventional design of trees, a balcony and water; the rest of the surface covered with a rich green glaze relieved by medallions in red and blue. Mark, *Taimin Banreki Nensei*. (Copied from the Chinese mark of the period Wanleih.) Date, 1750.

No. 16.—Shallow Dish, octagonal. Diameter, 10 in. Depth, 2¼ in.
>Richly decorated with floral subjects and pierced medallions. Date, 1730.

No. 17.—Plate, round. Diameter, 9½ in.
>Central design, red peonies with rich blue leaves on a white ground, surrounded by a deep border of green, red, and purple diapers, with medallions in red and blue. Date, 1700.

No. 18.—Plate, octagonal. Diameter, 8¼ in.
>Central design, a basket of flowers surrounded by a broad band of wave-pattern in gold on a blue ground, among which are circular diapers and bunches of leaves. Date, 1700.

No. 19.—Plate, hexagonal. Diameter, 8¾ in.
>Covered with a floral scroll, among which are medallions with diapers in rich glazes of many colors, very delicately executed. Date, 1730.

No. 20.—Plate, round. Diameter, 8¼ in.
>Central design, figure and floral subjects, round which is a band of rich red, with scroll pattern and medallions, and round this again a band of diapers. Date, 1780.

No. 21.—Bowl and Stand. Diameter, 8 in. Depth, 3½ in.

    Very richly decorated, the outside covered with deep red glaze in which are a dragon, a *Howo*, and clouds in blue, green, and yellow. Inside, a combination of various diapers, scrolls, and conventional designs. In the bottom the character *Ju* (congratulation) in gold on a red ground. Date, 1760.

No. 22.—Plate, peach-shaped. Diameter, 8¼ in.

    Centre crossed by irregularly shaped broad belt of red with floral scroll in gold. Round this are disposed diamond-shaped nests of diapers in various colors. Date, 1780.

No. 23.—Plate, octagonal. Diameter, 8¾ in.

    Decorated in panels each containing red medallions in which are circles of pierced wave-pattern and scroll designs. The medallions are separated by bands of blue and gold. The bottom has a chain of round medallions on a white ground. Mark *Hei* (Maker's name). Date, 1840.

No. 24.—Dish, square, with raised base. Side, 7½ in.

    Richly decorated with medallions and diapers. In the centre and at the corners the character *Ju* (congratulation). Date, 1790.

No. 25.—Bowl, round. Diameter, 8 in. Depth, 2¾ in.

    Outside, a green ground with *Howo* and dragon in white, gold, yellow and red. Inside, landscapes, clouds and purple and green diapers. Exceedingly delicately executed. Date, 1750.

No. 26.—Bowl, round. Diameter, 9¼ in. Depth, 3 in.

    Outside, a rich scroll. Inside, the central design is a carp and waves in blue, which is surrounded by a rich combination of scrolls in green and blue panels. Date, 1730.

No. 27.—Bowl, round. Diameter, 9½ in. Depth, 2½ in.

    Decorated outside with a band of leaves in blue on a white ground, above which is a broad band of diapers and medallions, the latter peach-shaped, their central design being the Sacred Jewel surrounded by flames. The bottom, inside, is decorated with a scroll of dragon and *Howo;* above this is a broad band of diapers and quaint medallions; and above this a band of wave pattern in blue, with fishes in red and gold, and formal medallions. A rare combination of designs. Date, 1760. Mark, *Taimin Banreki Nensei*. (Copied from the Chinese mark of the Wanleih period.)

No. 28.—Bowl, round. Diameter, 9 in. Depth, 2¾ in.

    Decorated outside with diapers of clouds and waves separating large red medallions with floral designs in white and gold. Inside, a rich combination of scrolls and medallions. Date, 1730. Mark, *Taimin Banreki Nensei*. (*Vide* No. 27.)

No. 29.—Bowl, round. Diameter, 11 in. Depth, 3½ in.

    Covered outside and inside with rich, red enamel, in which are medallions in deep blue, containing alternately landscapes and the character *Ju* (congratulation) disposed in a circular form. Date, 1700. Mark *Fuku* in a square.

No. 30.—Bowls, round, two. Diameter, 5¾ in. and 5½ in. respectively. Depth, 2 in.

    The outside a rich blue ground with scroll of peonies and vine tendrils in gold. Inside, a coiled dragon in blue and gold on the bottom, and on the sides rich red medallions separated by the design called *Yoraku-moyo*. The inside rim has a band of diapers in red. Date, 1760. Mark, *Taimin Kasei Nensei*. (Copied from the Chinese mark of the Keatsing period.) N. B.—Good specimens of this decoration are almost unprocurable.

No. 31.—Jar, with Cover. Height, 8½ in. Diameter, 6 in.

    Sides decorated with large medallions containing floral scrolls in green, yellow and purple on a rich red ground. The space between the medallions is covered with a diaper of interlacing diamonds in red, green and purple. On the body, under the neck, is a triple band of small hexagons with stars in various colors. The lid and neck decorated like the body. Date, 1730. Mark, *Taimin Banreki Nensei*. (*Vide* No. 27.)

No. 32.—Bowls, with Covers, two. Diameter, 5 in. Height, 4 in.

    Lid and body decorated with figure subjects and landscapes, delicately executed. Some of the figures are enclosed in circular medallions with rich red ground. Date, 1780. Mark, on lid and cover, *Banreki Nensei*. (*Vide* No. 22.)

No. 33.—Figure of woman in old-fashioned dress. Height, 18 in.

    Pattern of dress, floral designs in red, blue and gold. Date, 1720.

No. 34.—Scent-bottle, square in section. Height, 2 in., by 1⅛ in. square.

    Decorated with very delicately executed diapers in red enclosing white spaces with floral designs. Date, 1780.

No. 35.—Cylindrical vessel for holding tea-cloth. Height, 2½ in. Diameter, 1¼ in.

    Body covered with coral red glaze, on which are delicately executed dragons in gold. Above and below are bands of rich green diaper. Date, 1680. A rare specimen.

No. 36.—Water Holder. Height, 7½ in. Diameter, 7¼ in.

    Body decorated with 32 vertical strips of diapers in green, purple and red, among which are three circular medallions containing floral designs and birds in blue on a red ground. Between the medallions are fabulous animals (*Kirin*) in deep blue. Round the upper rim, inside and outside, are bands with floral scrolls on red ground. Date, 1760. Mark, *Fukki Choshun*. (*Vide* No. 14.)

No. 37.—Plate, square. Side, 6 in.
>Decoration, blue and red diapers with red and blue medallions. Date, 1750. Mark, *Taimin Banreki Nensei*. (*Vide* No. 27.)

No. 38.—Bottle, square. Height, 9 in. Side, 4 in.
>On the sides are delicately executed plums, pines, chrysanthemums, birds, &c., the panels which these occupy having blue borders with scrolls in gold. The upper surface is also covered with blue ground on which are butterflies and scrolls in gold, separated by four red leaves. The neck springs from a 42-petalled chrysanthemum. Date, 1790.

No. 39.—Bowl, with lid. Height, 1½ in. Diameter, 9½ in.
>Decoration, flights of sparrows in gold, purple and green, and medallions with bold leaf scrolls in blue and gold, on a rich red ground. Date, 1750.

No. 40.—Bowls, with lids, two. Diameter, 4¾ in. Height, 3¼ in.
>Round the upper and lower rims a band of green and red diaper. The rest of the decoration consists of incised designs in the white paste and circular red medallions with the character *Ju* (congratulation) in gold. An uncommon style of decoration. Date, 1780. Mark, *Fukki Choshun*. (*Vide* No. 14.)

No. 41.—Bottles, square, with rounded shoulders, two. Height, 8 in. Side, 3 in.
>Shoulders decorated with medallions and formal designs in green, red and gold. On the sides rich bands of red and blue scrolls enclose panels in which are floral and figure subjects. Date, 1800.

No. 42.—Bottle, square. Height, 9 in. Side, 3 in.
>In the centre of the sides are sunken panels with *Howo* and *shishi*. These panels are pierced by branches of cherry, plum, chrysanthemum, &c., the whole enclosed in bands of scrolls. The shoulder is covered with diapers and medallions. Date, 1780.

No. 43.—Bottle, square. Height, 9 in. Side, 4½ in.
>On the sides are sprays of plum and peony enclosed in rich borders of floral scrolls. The shoulders are decorated with floral sprays. Date, 1760.

No. 44.—Wine Bottles, two. Globular bodies with long tapering necks. Height, 8½ in. Diameter, 3½ in.
>Rich decoration of sprays and flowers with circular medallions of diapers on a pure white ground.

No. 45.—Incense-burner, rectangular, with perforated sides and top. Base, 4½ in. by 4 in. Body, 3¾ in. by 3 in. Height, 4½ in.
>The sides have triple lozenge-shaped panels with raised designs of pine trees and clouds, and scrolls on a red ground. Round the edges are delicate red diapers. Inner portion covered with rich diapers and medallions with floral designs. Date, 1750.

No. 46.—Incense-burner, with perforated lid and elephant heads for handles. Body, 3½ in. by 2½ in.. Height, 3½ in.

> Body covered completely with rich cherry petal diapers, except the upper halves of opposite sides which are white with delicate landscapes. Date, 1730.

No. 47.—Incense-burner.

> Same as No. 46, the landscapes only being replaced by dragons and clouds on a rich green ground. Date, 1740.

No. 48.—Incense-burner, general shape same as preceding. Sides, 3¼ in. and 2½ in. Height, 4 in.

> Sides decorated with flowers and butterflies, round which are bands of cherry-blossom diapers on red ground. The lid is perforated in shape of coiled dragon. Date, 1750.

No. 49.—Bowl, round. Diameter, 8¼. Depth, 2½.

> Outside, fishes in blue and red. Inside, on bottom, three *Howo* separated by medallions containing formal designs in gold on red ground. The sides decorated with rich combinations of diapers and medallions. Date, 1730.

No. 50.—Bowl, round. Diameter, 6½ in. Depth, 2½ in.

> Outside, simple scrolls of dragons and floral sprays on pure white ground. Inside, covered with very rich decoration, viz., on the bottom a *Shishi* in yellow and red entangled in a net with white meshes on a rich blue ground. Round this are disposed medallions with floral sprays and *Howo* on rich green ground. Date, 1750.

No. 51.—Bowl, round. Diameter, 6¼ in. Height, 2¼ in.

> Outside, decoration very slight, floral sprays in medallions and flowers. Inside covered with rich red glaze in which are medallions with floral subjects and between these the Sacred Jewel and flames in green. On the bottom a landscape. Date, 1780.

No. 52.—Bowl, round. Diameter, 11 in. Depth, 3 in.

> Outside, a scroll of chrysanthemums and *Aoi* leaves. Inside, a red ground with gold and white floral scroll springing from blue chrysanthemums and separating large medallions with floral designs: the bottom is white with a central design in blue, *Shishi* and peonies. Date, 1700. Mark, *Fuku* in square.

No. 53.—Bowl, round. Diameter, 5 in. Depth, 2½ in.

> Outside, a broad band of red between narrow bands of delicately executed diapers in blue, green and yellow. In the red band are circular medallions with tortoise, *Shishi, Howo* and *Kirin* in deep blue. Inside, design known as *Yoraku moyo*. On bottom, character *Ju* (congratulation). Date, 1750. Mark, *Reiken Chingan* (Rare toy).

No. 54.—Bowl, round. Diameter, 4¾ in. Height, 3½ in.

>Outside, covered with deep red enamel on which are figures of Eight Sages in gold, green and purple. Inside, floral sprays and landscape in blue. Date, 1700. Mark, leaves and scrolls.

No. 55.—Cups, cylindrical tapering, ten. Diameter, above 3 in., below, 1¾ in. Height, 2¼ in.

>Made to represent bundles of reeds, in blue, bound round the middle with double cord in red and gold, and decorated with cherry blossoms in red and gold. Date, 1760. Mark, *Fukki Choshun*. (*Vide* No. 14.)

No. 56.—Tea Jars, two. Height, 3 in. Diameter, 2 in.

>Covered with red diapers, among which are cherry petals and leaves, and large medallions containing floral sprays on a red ground. Date, 1820.

No. 57.—Bowls, fluted, with scolloped edges, five. General section, a square of 5¼ in. side. Depth, 2½ in.

>Richly decorated inside with red diapers and leaf-scrolls in green, separating medallions containing chrysanthemums in gold with blue leaves and sprays on a rich red ground. On the bottom, a floral scroll in a circular white space surrounded by a band of blue and gold. On the outside the design called *Yoraku-moyo*. Date, 1700.

No. 58.—Bowl, with Cover, and raised foot. Height, 7 in. Diameter, 5¾ in.

>Covered with diapers and medallions delicately executed in rich enamels. Round the base and top are bands of gold chrysanthemums on a purple ground. Date, 1750.

No. 59.—Water-holder. Height, 11½ in. Diameter, 15¼ in.

>Round the middle is a girdle of red with a scroll of peonies in white and gold, and medallions containing floral designs. The space below this girdle has a landscape in colors with medallions coning floral designs: the space above has a profusion of plums and pines. On the bottom inside is a coiled dragon among clouds. Date, 1760.

No. 60.—Water-holder. Height, 11¼ in. Diameter, 13½ in.

>Decoration, a large medallion with a deep black border, containing a hawk on a perch, with curtains overhead, in red, gold and black: the rest of the surface richly decorated with peonies and chrysanthemums. Date, 1780.

No. 61.—Bowl. Diameter, 10¼ in. Depth, 3¾ in.

>Fluted so as to represent a twenty-petalled chrysanthemum. On the bottom inside is a 24-petalled chrysanthemum in gold. The rest of the surface, inside and outside, is covered with diapers, scrolls and medallions. Date, 1780. Mark, *Taimin Banreki Nensei*. (*Vide* No. 27.)

No. 62.—Bowl, with cover. Height, 3¼ in. Diameter, 5 in.
> Covered with rich red enamel, among which are figures of the Eight Genii in coloured enamels. Date, 1780.

No. 63.—Incense-burner, cylindrical, with silver top. Height, 3 in. Diameter, 3 in.
> Body covered with rich red enamel on which are floral scrolls and three circular medallions, with delicately executed landscapes in rich enamels. Date, 1750.

No. 64.—Bowl. Diameter, 9¾ in. Depth, 4 in.
> Decorated outside with *Howo*, fabulous animals (*Kirin*) and conventional flames, in blue, red, purple, yellow, and green, forming a scroll: inside, with a diaper of squares in red, among which are medallions with floral subjects, and in the centre a *shishi* and leaves in blue. Date, 1780. Mark, *Taimin Banreki Nensei*. (*Vide* No. 27.)

No. 65.—Bowl, with cover. Diameter, 4 in. Height, 3 in.
> Milk white porcelain with sparse decoration of maple branches and leaves in blue, red and gold. Date, 1780.

No. 66.—Flower-pot. Height, 7½ in. Diameter, 10 in.
> Decorated in two bands of yellow with white intervening. On the yellow bands are waves, fishes and shells delicately executed. Date, 1800. A very uncommon species of decoration.

No. 67.—Incense-burner, round, with tapering base, silver legs and lid. Height, 3 in. Diameter, 2¾ in.
> The body is pierced in a design of storks among lotus leaves and flowers. The storks are covered with a white glaze, the lotus leaves and flowers with brown and red. Below are conventional waves in blue. The whole is dusted with globules of gold and silver. A very rare specimen. Date, 1780.

* No. 68.—Bowl. Diameter, 6 in. Depth, 3 in.
> Decorated outside with floral scrolls and medallions in green, yellow, red, and gold: inside with floral medallions on a deep blue ground. Mark, *Taimin Banreki Nensei*. (*Vide* No. 27.) Date, 1770.

No. 69.—Cup. Diameter, 3 in. Depth, 2½ in.
> Round the rim a band of squares enclosing chrysanthemums in blue under the glaze: below these a band of butterflies and scrolls picked out with red. Date, 1780.

No. 69A.—Wine Kettle, hexagonal, with spout and handle. Height, 7 in. Diameter, 5½ in.
> Covered with a diamond diaper in light yellow, blue, and gold, among which are medallions containing formal designs in red and blue on a gold ground. On the knob of the lid, and round the base of the knob is a chrysanthemum. Date, 1780. This specimen represents the very highest achievement of the Hizen potters.

---
* Not received from Japan. (E. G.)

No. 69B.—Bowl, with cover. Diameter, 11 in. Height, 9½ in.
> Richly decorated with medallions and floral designs. Date, 1780.

No. 69C.—Figure of Warrior in Armour, seated. Height, 13¼ in.
> The face is unglazed; the armour, in coloured enamels. Date, 1670.

No. 69D.—Jar, with cover. Height, 15½ in. Diameter, 8 in.
> The lid and neck are decorated with scrolls and medallions of chrysanthemum flowers and leaves. Round the shoulder is a broad band of blue, covered with leaf scrolls in gold, among which are large heart-shaped medallions containing chrysanthemum leaves and flowers, and between the medallions are chrysanthemums in red. The body is white, with chrysanthemum flowers and leaves in blue, red, and gold. Date, 1750.

IMARI BLUE AND WHITE PORCELAIN.

"*The decoration here described is that known as blue under the glaze. Blue thus applied enters into the decoration of all the enamelled porcelain produced in Hizen, with the exception of the wares of Kakiyemon and his imitators. The decoration with vitrifiable enamels was a process subsequent to the stoving of the glazed piece, and was, in fact, added to a vase which, without it, would have been a finished specimen of blue-and-white. To vitrify and fix the enamels another stoving was required.*"—From BRINKLEY's *History of Japanese Keramics.*

No. 70.—Incense-box, elliptical with straight ends. 3 in. by 2½ in.
> Design, *Takara-dzukushi* in white on a blue ground. Date, 1820.

No. 71.—Incense-box, clove shaped. 3 in. by 3 in.
> The sides covered with diapers; the top decorated with two *Howo* and bands of diamonds enclosing chrysanthemum petals. Date, 1800.

No. 72.—Nest of Ten Cups. Largest, diameter, 4¾ in., depth, 3 in. Smallest, diameter, 2¼ in., depth, ½ in.
> Design, a group of pines, plums, and bamboos, opposite which is a large medallion enclosing a landscape; in the intervening space are two circles of diapers and a bat. Date, 1800.

No. 73.—Jar. Height, 3 in. Diameter, 2¾ in.

*   Decoration, a rich blue ground on which are plums, bamboos, pines, and sparrows in white. Date, 1750.

No. 74.—Pen-rest, rectangular, 3 in. by 1¾ in. Height, 1 in.

The centre is pierced in lattice design, the remainder, covered with various diapers. Date, 1800.

No. 75.—Water-holder, cylindrical. Height, 6½ in. Diameter, 6½ in.

Covered with peonies and *shishi*. Date, 1780.

No. 76.—Incense-burner, cylindrical. Height, 2½ in. Diameter, 2½ in.

Design, delicately painted landscapes. Mark, *Tsuji Hitachi Chikatsune Seisu* (made by Tsuji Chikatsune, whose artist rank was Hitachi). Date, 1820.

No. 77.—Incense-burner, globular, body pierced in form of peony blossom and leaves, with tripod stand. Height, 8½ in. Diameter, 4½ in.

The body is pure white, the top, surmounted by a blue lion (*shishi*). The stand is covered with diapers and floral designs. Date, 1780.

No. 78.—Bottle, gourd-shaped. Height, 7½ in.

Decoration, seven children at play. Date, 1800.

No. 79.—Flower Vase, gourd-shaped. Height, 4 in.

Covered with delicately pencilled diapers scattered among clouds and flames in which are floating four-clawed dragons. Mark round the neck *Kai-sui Yen daisu* (painted by Kai-sui Yen). Same mark on bottom. Date, 1800.

* Not received from Japan. (E. G.)

HIRADO, BLUE AND WHITE, PORCELAIN.

"The factory at Mikôchi-yama (written *Mikawa-uchi-yama*, or the 'hill between the three rivers'), like that at Okôchi, was taken under special patronage. It appears that one at least of the potters who came to Japan in the train of Hideyoshi's generals settled at Mikôchi, about the year 1595, and inaugurated the manufacture of faience decorated with blue under the glaze. No specimens of this ware are believed to be now extant. We may presume that it did not deserve preservation. Some twenty years later, the porcelain clay discovered by Risampei, came into use at Mikôchi, but, the method of applying vitrifiable enamels not being known, the only colour employed for decorative purposes was blue under the glaze. Probably for this reason the industry did not flourish, and the workshops had long been closed when, about the year 1740, Matsura, feudal chief of Hirado, an island off the coast of Hizen, caused them to be re-opened and placed the workmen under strict supervision, forbidding them to sell or dispose of their productions without special permission. This nobleman appears to have been a very practical connoisseur. He bestowed scarcely less attention on the potteries of his fief than Louis XV. did on those of Sèvres. The pieces turned out were reserved entirely for his own use and that of his friends, or for presentation to the Court of the Tokugawa Regents in Yedo. To the ware potted at Mikôchi from this time (1740) until the period of Tempo (1830) must unquestionably be assigned the first place among the porcelains of Japan. It is called *Hirado yaki*. The *pâte*, finer, purer and whiter than that of either *Nabeshima-yaki* or *Imari-yaki*, owed its exceptional qualities entirely to careful manipulation. On the trituration of the clay and its subsequent washing and straining, pains almost unlimited were bestowed, and the preparation of the glazing material was the work of months. Examined attentively, the *pâte* is found to be virtually free from the dark gritty particles so common in Imari ware, and the granulations in the surface of the glaze, invisible to the naked eye, are not more marked than in the best Chinese porcelain. It is not, however, till we consider the decoration that the incomparable beauties of this *Hirado-yaki* become fully apparent. With rare exceptions, blue is the only colour employed. It is not the intense, fathomless colour of the old Chinese Keramists, nor yet is it the light, bodiless blue of the Nabeshima ware. It is a colour between the two, exquisitely soft and clear, and harmonizing perfectly with the milk-white, velvet-like glaze in which it seems to float. Of the execution of the designs it is impossible to speak too highly. Nothing approaching them can be found in the whole range of Chinese porcelains. One is puzzled to conceive, in the first place, how etching so wonderfully fine and outlines of such detailed accuracy can have been transferred to a surface of baked clay, and, in the second, how every process of glazing and stoving can have been effected with sufficient skill to preserve these delicate pictures. There are few subjects which the artists of Mikôchi did not depict upon their pieces, and fewer still in which they fell short of marked success." " It is very doubtful whether many really choice specimens of *Hirado-yaki* have yet found their way westward. Only within the last five years did the passion for blue-and-white, suddenly developed in Europe, induce Japanese virtuosi to place this ware upon the market, and the supply, always very limited, did not last long enough to familiarize American and European collectors with the merits of Japan's best porcelain."—From BRINKLEY'S *History of Japanese Keramics.*

No. 80.—Flower vase, globular body, with spreading neck and elephant-head handles. Height, 12½ in. Diameter of neck, 9¾ in.

> Body covered with delicately painted landscapes; the upper rim with a diaper. Date, 1750.

No. 81.—Water-holder, cylindrical, made to imitate a section of bamboo. Height, 8 in. Diameter, 6½ in.

> Decoration, the Seven Sages in a Bamboo Grove. Date, 1760.

No. 82.—Cake-box, cylindrical, with tapering base. Height, 10 in. Diameter, 6 in.

> Round the base is a band of waves, raised in the paste; round the body, a flight of storks in blue; the lid is surmounted by a tortoise. Date, 1780.

No. 83.—Water-holder, cylindrical. Height, 7 in. Diameter, 5¾ in.

> Covered with a boldly executed leaf scroll. Date, 1800.

No. 84.—Water-holder, square above and circular below, Height, 7 in. Diameter, 6 in.

> Decoration, a clump of bamboos. Date, 1780.

No. 85.—Incense-burner, cylindrical, with open-work top. Height, 3 in. Diameter, 2½ in.

> Decoration, five children at play, and landscape. Date, 1760.

No. 86.—Incense-burner, cylindrical, with open-work top and three feet. Height, 2½ in. Diameter, 2¾ in.

> Round the upper rim is a scroll of leaves and flowers. The body is decorated with tree subjects. Date, 1760.

No. 87.—Incense-burner, cylindrical with open-work top, and globular body. Height, 3 in. Diameter, 3 in.

> Decoration, delicately executed landscapes. Date, 1820.

No. 88.—Incense-burner, cylindrical, with open-work top. Height, 3½ in. Diameter, 3 in.

> Decoration, petals of cherry-blossoms. Date, 1780.

No. 89.—Wine Bottle, with globular body and narrow neck. Height, 8 in. Diameter, 5 in.

> Figure subjects and landscape delicately executed. Date, 1800.

No. 90.—Wine Bottle, tapering body and narrow neck. Height, 8 in. Diameter, 5 in.

Delicately executed landscapes. Date, 1760.

No. 91.—Vase, gourd-shaped with narrow neck. Height, 4 in. Diameter, 2¼ in.

Design, trees, rocks and children at play. Date, 1800.

No. 92.—Scent Bottle, gourd shaped with narrow neck. Height, 3 in. Diameter, 1¾ in.

Design, floral subjects and leaf scrolls. Date, 1800.

No. 93.—Plate. Diameter, 9¼ in.

Decoration, outside a floral scroll; inside, five medallions with *Tokugawa mon*, the intervening spaces occupied by willow boughs. Date, 1800.

No. 94.—Bowl. Diameter, 7¾ in. Depth, 3 in.

Design, crabs in various positions, delicately painted. Date, 1780.

No. 95.—Wine Vessel, with bamboo handle. Height (without handle), 4 in. Diameter, 5½ in.

Design, delicately executed landscapes. Date, 1800.

No. 96.—Wine Vessel. Height, 7 in. Diameter, 4½ in.

Design, delicately executed landscapes. Date, 1820.

No. 97.—Clove-boiler, with pierced lid. Height, 7½ in. Diameter, 7 in.

Decoration, grains of rice pattern, each grain raised in the paste and filled with blue enamel. Date, 1750.

No. 98.—Water-holder in form of Sparrow. Height, 3 in. Distance across wings, 4½ in.

On the back are plums, bamboos, and pines raised in the paste, and very delicately executed. Date, 1780.

No. 99.—Flower-holder for hanging on wall, cylindrical. Height, 5 in. Diameter, 2 in.

Decoration, plum-blossoms raised in the paste and a diaper. Date, 1750.

No. 100.—Flower-vase, bottle-shaped. Height, 5½ in. Diameter, 1¾ in.

Decorated with landscapes. Date, 1820.

No. 101.—Plate, in the form of a peony leaf. Diameter, 7¼ in.

Decoration, three butterflies. Date, 1780.

No. 102.—Vase, with globular body and spreading neck. Height, 13 in. Diameter above, 11½ in.

> On the lower part of the body are conventional waves; from the inside a profusion of willow branches droops over the edges. The handles are in the form of frogs. Date, 1760.

No. 103.—Group of Three Children playing Drafts. Dimensions of base, 5 in. by 3½ in. Height, 2½ in.

> The dresses of the children are in blue. Date, 1780.

No. 104.—Incense-burner, with round base and conical top. Height, 3½ in. Diameter of base, 3¼ in.

> Decoration, trees, and children at play. The top has four circles of pierced pattern delicately cut and unglazed. Date, 1760.

No. 105.—Incense-burner, in form of Tortoise, with Genius riding on it. Height, 5 in. Length, 8 in.

> The teeth and eyes of the tortoise and face of Genius are unglazed; the feet and head of the Genius are covered with chocolate-coloured glaze. Date, 1780.

No. 106.—Plate. Diameter, 8½ in.

> Round the rim outside, a band of comb's teeth. The upper surface divided into three irregular spaces containing plum, pine, and bamboo designs. Date, 1760.

No. 107.—Cylindrical Ash-holder. Height, 3½ in. Diameter, 2½ in.

> Decoration, delicately executed landscapes in deep blue. Date, 1760.

No. 107A.—Water-holder, cylindrical. Diameter, 6 in. Height, 8 in.

> Decoration, three *Sen-nin*, pine-tree, and landscape. Date, 1790.

EGG-SHELL BLUE AND WHITE PORCELAIN,

MIKÔUCHI KILN.

"The Mikôchi potters, like their neighbours of Okôchi, did not mark their pieces, until a very late period of the manufacture (1830-1843). An exception to this is the Hirado egg-shell porcelain, on the under surface of which we generally find the ideographs *Zôshuntei Sampô-sei*, signifying 'made by Sampo at the factory Zôshun.'"—From BRINKLEY's *History of Japanese Keramics*.

No. 108.—Bowl, with Cover and Stand. Diameter, 5 in. Height, 3½ in.

    Design, carp and water grasses. Date, 1820. Mark, *Zôshuntei Sampô-sei* (Made by Sampo at the Kiln called Zôshun).

No. 109.—Shallow Bowl. Diameter, 5 in. Depth, 1¼ in.

    Design, floral scroll, lantern and medallion with birds. Date, 1820.

No. 110.—Cups, six. Diameter, 3¾ in. Depth, 2 in.

    Decoration, eight vertical bands with floral subjects. Date, 1820. Mark, *Zôshuntei Sampo-sei* (*Vide* No. 108).

No. 111.—Bowl, with Cover and Stand. Diameter, 3¾ in. Height, 3½ in.

    Decoration, panels with floral subjects and birds, landscape and verses of poetry. Mark, *Zoshuntei Sampo-sei* (*Vide* No. 108). Date, 1820.

No. 111A.—Cup. Diameter, 4 in. Depth, 1½ in.

    Decorated with delicately executed plum blossoms and three medallions of *Tokugawa mon*. Date, 1830.

WHITE HIRADO PORCELAIN.

"We find the potter setting himself technical tasks, like those in which his Chinese confrère revelled. He would enclose a tiny censer in a basket of porcelain, or spread over the surface of a milk white glaze designs in relief, executed with mechanical and artistic fidelity superior even to the work of the Chinese. He delighted, too, in modelling little figures of his favorite *Karuko*, rampant dragons, mythical *Shishi*, wrinkled old men, fishes, and so forth. In this sort of work he excelled all other porcelain manufacturers in the Orient. Vitrifiable enamels he used scarcely at all, but in the drapery of his *Karuko*, and other models, we find three coloured glazes, rich blue, russet-brown and black."—From BRINKLEY'S *History of Japanese Keramics*.

No. 112.—Water-holder, cylindrical, with Cover. Height, 8 in. Diameter, 6 in.

    Round the body, above and below, are bands of basket-work pattern, and between them, delicately moulded peonies and leaves, in relief. Date, 1780.

No. 113.—Bottle, gourd-shaped. Height, 8 in. Diameter, 4½ in.
    Design, delicately executed chrysanthemums and leaves in relief. Date, 1780.

No. 114.—Dragon. Length, 6¼ in. Height, 3 in. Date, 1820.

No. 115.—Incense-burner, in the form of Devil, seated. Height, 4 in. Date, 1750.

No. 116.—Incense-burner, circular. Height, 3 in. Diameter, 3 in.
    Sides and top exceedingly delicate open-work, with two circular panels containing the *Tokugawa mon*. Date, 1750.

No. 117.—Pen-holder, in the form of Three Osier Baskets forming a river-dam, on which are Two Tortoises. Length, 7 in. Height, 1½ in. Date, 1780.

No. 118.—Lion, *couchant*. Length, 3¼ in. Height, 2 in. Date, 1820.

No. 119.—Lion with Ball. Height, 1½ in. Length, 1 in. Date, 1750.

No. 120.—Paper-weight, circular. Diameter, 2 in.
    Delicately modelled chrysanthemums on a conventional stand. Date, 1820.

No. 121.—Rabbit. Length, 7½ in. Height, 5 in. Date, 1820.

No. 122.—Lion with Ball. Length, 8 in. Height, 7½ in. Date, 1800.

No. 123.—Incense-burner, in the form of Baku (Genius of nightmares). Height, 6 in. Length, 5½ in. Date, 1780.

No. 124.—Dragon. Length, 2½ in. Height, 2½ in. Date, 1800.

No. 124A.—Figures of Takeda Shingen and Uyesugi Kenshin. Height of former 8 in., of latter 14½ in. Date, 1820.

HIRADO PORCELAIN WITH COLOURED ENAMELS.

No. 125.—Flower Vase in the shape of a Clump of Bamboos, at the base of which are the Seven Sages. Height, 10 in. Base, 8 by 10 in.

> The foliage of the bamboos is in blue; the bamboos themselves are a light green, and the dresses of the Sages are blue and russet brown. Date, 1700.

No. 126.—Incense-burner, the God Hotei sitting on a Bag and holding a Wine-gourd. Height, 5 in. Diameter of bag, 6¾ in.

> The figure's drapery is blue and russet brown, the face and breast unglazed. Date, 1700.

No. 127.—Genius with Wine-gourd. Height, 4½ in. Date, 1840.

No. 128.—Eagle on Rock. Height, 9 in.

> The rock is brown with greenish moss, the bird white. Date, 1820.

No. 129.—Wine-holder. Diameter, 4¾ in. Height, 3 in.

> White chrysanthemums and blue leaves in relief on a rich brown ground. Date, 1840.

No. 130.—Wine Bottles, two. Height, 7 in.

> Ivory white with straw-coloured rope and tassels round the shoulder. Date, 1700.

WHITE HIZEN PORCELAIN.

(OF THIS VARIETY VERY FEW SPECIMENS EXIST.)

No. 131.—Wine Bottle, with hexagonal base and indented sides.

> The ground is made so as to present a sponge-like appearance. On the shoulder are sunken panels with floral designs in relief. On the body a tiger stands on a rock from which a plum tree grows, while over-head a dragon emerges from the clouds. These subjects are in relief. Round the base is a band of panels with archaic designs. Date, 1700.

NABESHIMA PORCELAIN.

DECORATED WITH COLOURED ENAMELS AND BLUE UNDER THE GLAZE.

"Among the twenty porcelain factories of Hizen, forming a group in the neighbourhood of Imari, two have been reserved for special mention. They are Okôchi-yama and Mikôchi-yama. Okôchi-yama—which is written ' O-kawa-uchi-yama,' or ' the hill within the great river '—is remarkable as having been established by Nabeshima, feudal chief of Hizen, in 1716, who gave orders that the wares produced there should be reserved entirely for use in his own castle or for presentation to his friends. The pieces made there escaped the influence of the Dutch traders, and the decoration employed was governed entirely by the canons of Japanese taste. The ornamentation is consequently less profuse than that of the *Imari-yaki*, and the ware altogether is characterized by chasteness and delicacy. The *pâte* is finer and whiter, with less admixture of foreign particles than that of the ' Old Japan,' though in some very excellent specimens it has a marked tinge of red. The glaze also is distinguished by purity and lustre : examined carefully it shows minute pitting similar to that seen in the porcelain of Imari, but of the two the granulation of the former will be found less marked. The most strikingly distinctive feature of the Nabeshima porcelain is that decoration in blue under the glaze is relegated to a subordinate place." "The Nabeshima potters, as a rule, did not use marks, and never copied Chinese marks except on pieces which were obvious reproductions of Chinese originals. The reason of this is easily understood when we remember that the productions of the Okôchi factories were destined solely for the House of Nabeshima. Okôchi, in fact, was a private kiln. There was no occasion to mark porcelains manufactured there as though they were intended for general sale. With the rare exception, therefore, of the ideograph *Fuku* (No. 138 of this collection), *Nabeshima-yaki* may be said to be without marks or seals of any description."—From BRINKLEY'S *History of Japanese Keramics.*

No. 132.—Plates, two. Diameter, 12¼ in.

    The central subjects are figures in a garden. The rest of the surface is divided by double red lines into 8 panels in which are various floral and figure subjects. Colors, red, green, yellow, and blue. Date, 1780.

No. 133.—Incense-burner, square with pierced lid and sides. Height, 4 in. Side, 3 in.

    Body covered with delicately executed chrysanthemums and leaves extending partially over the lid. Date, 1780.

No. 134.—Incense-burner, dome-shaped, with sides and lid pierced in Genji crest. Height, 3 in. Diameter, 3¾ in.

>Design, the seven flowers of autumn. Date, 1820.

No. 135.—Bowl. Diameter, 8¼ in. Depth, 3¾ in.

>External decoration, bamboos and plums with birds; internal, three coiled dragons, between which are floral sprays. Date, 1780.

No. 136.—Plate. Diameter, 8 in.

>Design, two quails with ears of corn, bamboo, plums, and bird. Round the outside is a floral scroll. Date, 1800.

No. 137.—Cake-holder, cylindrical, in two sections. Height, 5 in. Diameter, 4¼ in.

>From the three feet stretch upward three blue cords forming a knot with tassels in the centre of the lid. The lower half is sparsely decorated with floral designs, the upper is vertically divided by black rims into thirty spaces containing conventional floral scrolls. The lid is covered with a red meshed net. Date, 1780.

No. 138.—Large, deep Plate. Diameter, 14¾ in. Depth, 3¼ in.

>Richly decorated inside and outside with floral scrolls, flowers and trees. Date, 1800. Mark *Fuku* in a square.

No. 139.—Plates, with raised base, five. Diameter, 4½ in.

>External decoration, floral sprays in blue; internal, conventional waves in blue and white, among which are two fan-shaped spaces containing floral designs in red and blue. Date, 1780.

No. 140.—Incense-burner, basket-shaped. Diameter, 3¼ in. Depth, 2½ in.

>Thick stone-ware covered with a green glaze boldly crackled. Over the glaze are roughly executed floral designs in red, green, purple, and gold. Date, 1670. (From the collection of Ninagawa Noritane.)

No. 141.—Figure of Shinno, the first physician of Chinese tradition. Height, 4 in.

>The face, head and legs of the figure are unglazed; the mantle of oak leaves is in brown and blue glazes. Date, 1820.

NABESHIMA CELADON (LIGHT GREEN GLAZE).

"Special mention must be made of the celadon manufactured at the Okôchi factories. Elsewhere in Japan there have never been produced any such imitations of the finest Chinese ware. The colour of the glaze, in some of the best pieces, is indescribably beautiful, and one needs an eye exceptionally educated to perceive that, in point of purity and lustre, the advantage is with the Chinese original. The *pâte* of this Nabeshima celadon is of a light red colour in the oldest pieces, but in vases manufactured at the end of the eighteenth and beginning of the nineteenth century we find the ordinary white clay (*shiro-tsuchi*) of Idzumiyama."—From BRINKLEY'S *History of Japanese Keramics*.

No. 142.—Bottle, gourd shaped. Height, 12 in. Diameter, 6 in.
    Divided by spiral lines into six spaces. Date, 1750.

No. 143.—Vase, with globular body and spreading neck. Height, 13 in. Diameter, about 11 in.
    Round the base is a band of archaic figures under the glaze. On the sides are four elliptical panels with key patterns and archaic designs. Date, 1740.

No. 144.—Incense-burner, globular. Diameter, 3 in. Height, 2 in.
    Date, 1760.

SATUSMA FAIENCE.

"Whatever title to Keramic celebrity Japan may found upon her porcelain, it is probably for her pottery that she will be longest spoken of. For while her porcelain manufacturers—those of Hirado excepted—were always more or less subservient to the fashions of Chinese originals, her workers in pottery and faience gave untrammeled play to their native genius, and both in shapes and styles of decoration produced pieces of the greatest beauty and quaintness. Among all the faiences of Japan, Western amateurs have agreed to assign the first place to the well-known *Satsuma-yaki*. One may safely say that no European and American collection is deemed complete unless it contains a piece of the ware, and to this we are disposed to add—though few will be disposed to believe it—that Western collectors rarely possess a really respresentative specimen. It may not be denied that pottery of a brilliantly decorative, and at the same time artistic, nature has been exported in considerable quantities to Europe and America during the past ten years, under the name of old Satsuma, but there need be no hesitation in asserting that in many and most essential respects this showy ware differs completely from the beautiful faience so highly prized by Japanese connoisseurs. If it be admitted that first-class specimens of ancient Chinese celadon bear some comparison with the jade which they were designed to imitate, there will be no risk of hyperbole in asserting that the Satsuma ware of by-gone times can scarcely at first sight be distinguished from ivory."

"In 1598 the celebrated Shimazu Yoshihiro, Chieftain of Satsuma, returning from the invasion of Korea, brought with him a large number of workmen—some five score, it is said—of whom seventeen were skilled potters. They were settled at first in three villages, Kushikino, Ichiku, and Sanno-gawa; but subsequently a few of the most skilled among them were removed to Chôsa, in the neighbouring province of Osumi, where their patron, Yoshihiro, had one of his castles. Here ware of various sorts was produced: some copied directly from Korean models; some covered with glaze of various colours, green, yellow or black, and some of a *flambé* description. The paste was fine and well manipulated, and of a grayish red colour, but the chief beauty of the ware, or rather of the parti-coloured and *flambé* varieties, was the glaze, of which two, three, and sometimes four, coats were applied, until effects of considerable richness and diversity were obtained. A potter called Saburohei (*Vide* No. 166 of this collection) was especially renowned in this matter of glaze. His pieces bear no mark, but connoisseurs profess ability to distinguish them at once by their excellence of shape and lustrous surface."

"About the year 1670 Mitsuhisa, then Chief of Sasshiu, caused a kiln to be set up in the grounds of his own castle, and the workmen employed there were familiar with the use of vitrifiable enamels. Iyemitsu, third Regent of the Tokugawa Dynasty, had encouraged the already growing taste for highly decorated ware, and his influence was felt at all the centres of Keramic industry in Japan. The Prince of Sasshiu, having established a factory, invited thither the painter Tangen, pupil of the renowned Tanyu, and commissioned him either to paint faience himself or to furnish the workmen with designs. The outcome of this factory was necessarily small, the pieces being destined entirely for private use or for presents. But, that enamelled faience was produced there, and that beautiful specimens—known to this day as *Satsuma-Tangen*, from the name of the artist engaged in their decoration—are among the treasures of Japanese collectors, there is no valid reason to doubt. The point to be observed is that this fashion of decoration did not at that time extend to any other factory in the province. Thus, when the successors of Prince Mitsuhisa ceased to patronize the art, and when the private kiln established by that nobleman was closed, a considerable period elapsed before the potters of Tatsuno thought of studying processes which no longer received the encouragement of the lords of the district. At the end of the eighteenth century, however, Nari Akihira (afterwards called Yeiô), Chief of Sasshiu, took the factory at Tatsuno under its protection. It was at his instance that the two workmen, Kin and Kuwabara, visited Kyôto, and it is to his patronage that we owe the *rénaissance*, afterwards erroneously described as the origin, of Satsuma enamelled faience.

"The distinguishing feature of the specimens produced in the time of Yeiô, as well as in the early days of the manufacture, was the fineness of the *pâte*. It was as close-grained as pipe-clay, and almost as hard as porcelain biscuit. The Satsuma potter confined himself strictly to diapers, floral subjects, landscapes, and a few conventionalities, such as the *Howo*, the *Shishi* (mythical lion), the *Dragon* and the *Kirin* (unicorn).

"Although the faience of Satsuma is known to Western collectors chiefly for the sake of its enamelled pieces, its monochrome and *flambé* glazes also deserve mention. Of the former, yellow, and black (*vide* No. 166 of this collection) are the most remarkable, but both are exceedingly rare. Another monochrome glaze, which may almost be called a specialty of the Satsuma potters, is olive green (*vide* No 167 of this collection). This colour, however, is seldom employed alone, being generally associated with a peculiar dark mustard yellow, or a chocolate brown. Such glazes as these are for the most part confined to tea-jars, incense-boxes, and other utensils for use at *Cha no Yu* ceremonials. Neither is the *pâte* of pieces thus decorated made of the well-known white earth, but of an exceedingly fine iron-red pipe-clay, which the amateur easily learns to recognize after he has seen one or two specimens. Another infallible guide in identifying a Satsuma tea-jar (*chatsubo*) is the *ito-giri*; a mark left on the bottom by the thread with which the potter used to sever the piece from the clay out of which it was modelled. This mark is found upon all carefully manufactured Japanese tea-jars, but since the Korean workmen who settled in Satsuma turned the throwing-wheel with the left foot, while potters at other factories turned it with the right, it will be readily understood that the spiral of the Satsuma thread-mark is from left to right, and that of other factories from right to left. Pure white faience, sometimes cleverly moulded or reticulated, was a favorite production of the ancient Satsuma potters."—From BRINKLEY'S *History of Japanese Keramics*.

No. 145.—Incense-burner, cylindrical body with spreading base. Height, 8 in. Diameter, 4½ in.

    Round the juncture of the body and base is a double band of key pattern. On opposite sides are two rectangular panels containing pierced floral designs. On the top is a lion. Date, 1720.

No. 146.—Wine-holder, with spout and handle. Height, 6 in.

    Decorated with chrysanthemum flowers and leaves in red and gold. Date, 1800.

No. 147.—Vase, with spreading base and tapering neck. Height, 6½ in. Diameter, 3¾ in.

    Decoration, bunches of grass and medallions with floral subjects and diapers. Date, 1810.

No. 148.—Dish, oblong. Sides, 6 in. by 4 in. Depth, 1½ in.

    External decoration, floral scrolls; internal, peonies and leaves, with a band of diapers on the upper rim. Date, 1810.

No. 149.—Incense-holder in the form of a clam shell. Dimensions, 4¼ in. by 3½ in.

    The shell is unglazed, but on the upper and lower valves are chrysanthemum flowers, in relief, in white *engobe* picked out with gold. Date, 1730.

No. 150.—Vase, square in section with tapering base. Height, 5¼ in. Side of square, 2 in.

    The sides decorated with floral subjects: the shoulders and neck with scrolls and diapers. A piece has been broken off the base and replaced with Kyoto faience. Date, 1720.

No. 151.—Bonbon box, with Cover, round. Height, 4 in. Diameter, 3½ in.

    Decorated with pictures of the various musical instruments. Date, 1820.

No. 152.—Cup. Diameter 3¾ in. Depth, 2 in.

    Floral decoration. Date, 1830.

No. 153.—Paper weight in form of camelia leaves and bud. Length, 6½ in.

    Covered with a green and blue glaze. Date, 1810.

No. 154.—Wine-holder, with spout and handle. Height, 4½ in. Diameter, 3½ in.

    Delicate floral decoration with diapers round spout, handle, and top. Date, 1840.

(32)

No. 155.—Bonbon Box, with Lid, round. Diameter, 5 in. Height, $3\frac{1}{2}$ in.
> Decoration, bands of key pattern and floral medallions. Date, 1800.

No. 156.—Wine-holder, with spout and handle; octagonal body and cylindrical neck. Height, 5 in. Diameter, 3 in.
> Decoration, floral medallions. Date, 1810.

No. 157.—Incense-holder, round, with Lid. Diameter, $2\frac{1}{2}$ in.
> Delicate floral decoration. Date, 1840.

No. 158.—Saké Bottle, with spout and handle. Height, $5\frac{1}{2}$ in. Diameter, $4\frac{3}{4}$ in.
> Plain white. Date, 1840.

No. 159.—Incense-burner, in the form of Shoki, the Demon-slayer. Height, 11 in.
> His boots, edges of drapery, beard and head-dress are covered with black glaze; the rest of the figure is cream white. Date, 1820.

No. 160.—Vase, with tapering neck and handles. Height, 13 in.
> Ivory white. Date, 1700.

No. 161.—Incense-burner, with Silver Lid. Height, 3 in. Diameter, $2\frac{1}{2}$ in.
> Decoration, on body, floral subjects; round neck, a band of diapers. Date, 1830.

No. 162.—Cup. Diameter, $5\frac{1}{4}$ in. Height, 2 in.
> Decorated with interlacing medallions of flowers. Date, 1820. (From collection of Ninagawa Noritane.)

No. 163.—Cup. Diameter, 4 in. Height, $3\frac{3}{4}$ in.
> Divided vertically by spiral lines into spaces filled with delicately executed floral decoration and diapers. Date, 1830.

No. 164.—Tea Jar. Height, 3 in. Diameter, $2\frac{1}{4}$ in.
> Covered with iron red glaze over which is run a golden brown. Date, 1700.

No. 165.—Vase, square. Height, $7\frac{1}{2}$ in. Side, $4\frac{1}{2}$ in.
> Iron red glaze over which is run a black glaze flecked with blue and white. Date, 1780.

No. 166.—Tea Jar. Height, $2\frac{1}{2}$ in. Diameter, $2\frac{1}{2}$ in.
> Covered with mirror black glaze. Date, 1650. Made by Saburohei. (From the collection of Ninagawa Noritane.) *Tachino-yaki.*

No. 167.—Tea Jar. Height, 3 in. Diameter, 2¼ in.
>Covered with olive green glaze. Date, 1700.

No. 168.—Tea Jar. Height, 3½ in. Diameter, 2 in.
>Rich brown glaze flecked with blue. *Riumonji-yaki.* Date, 1700. (From the collection of Ninagawa Noritane.)

No. 169.—Tea Jar, with Bronze and Ivory Lids. Height, 2½ in. Diameter, 3 in.
>Decorated with bands of medallions and diapers. Date, 1810.

No. 170.—Tea Jar. Height, 2½ in. Diameter, 2¼ in.
>Decorated with vertical and horizontal bands of diapers. Remarkably fine paste and crackle. Date, 1800.

No. 171.—Large Vase, with cover. Height, 17 in. Diameter, 12½ in.
>Decoration, sprays of plum, bamboo, and pine. Date. 1800.

No. 172.—Bowl. Diameter, 4¼ in. Depth, 2¾ in.
>Divided by vertical yellow lines into spaces covered with brown, blue, gold and green enamels: on the bottom inside are four chrysanthemums in gold, and round the bottom outside three. Date, 1840.

No. 172A.—Vase. Height, 3¾ in. Diameter, 4 in.
>A brown glaze, over which is run a soft lilac. Round the body is a broad band (divided by six projecting ribs) of diapers, flowers and lines in metallic brown. Date, 1810. [Made to imitate a ware called, in Japan, *Sunkoroku*, and said to be of Persian origin.]

No. 172B.—Vase. Height, 5½ in. Diameter, 2½ in.
>A transparent greenish glaze clouded with blue, and decorated with black lines and diapers, and metallic spots. Date, 1810.

FAIENCE OF KYÔTÔ AND ENVIRONS.
SPECIMENS BY NOMURA NINSEI.

"With Nomura Seisuke (called also Seiyemon and Seibei) the real history of Kyôtô faience commences. There is no name more renowned in the catalogue of Japanese Keramists." "His native place was a village near the shrine of Ninwaji (pronounced Ninnaji) in the environs of Kyôtô, and by combining the initial syllable of this word with that of his name (Seisuke) there was obtained the term 'Ninsei,' by which the man and his works alike are known to posterity."

"Our readers will remember that the methods of decoration with vitrifiable enamels was acquired by Tokuzayemon, of Arita, in 1648. Naturally a considerable quantity of the new ware found its way to the capital, where it excited at once the admiration and envy of the leading Keramists. But for a time the possibility of imitating it does not seem to have been conceived, since the secret was guarded at the Hizen factories by a series of the most rigorous enactments. It happened, however, that, between the years 1650 and 1654, a certain Aoyama Koyemon, acting as agent for the sale of the new porcelain, associated himself with one Kuhei, a faience vendor of Kyôtô, and was pursuaded by the latter, who seems to have been gifted with no small amount of tact and craft, to disclose the methods which had won for Arita so valuable a monopoly. The unfortunate Koyemon's indiscretion is said to have cost him his life, but the precious recipe remained in Kuhei's possession, and subsequently passed into the hands of Nomura Ninsei. We may, therefore, with very little risk of inaccuracy, ascribe the first manufacture of enamelled faience in Japan to the year 1653.

"Not having made Keramics his profession, Ninsei had no fixed workshop. His first productions were potted in the neighbourhood of the temple of Seikan, and at a kiln called Otowa, both of which are in the district of Omuro. Hence the origin of the term *Omuro-yaki*, by which these pieces are generally known. Subsequently he worked at the factories of Awata, Iwakura, and Mizoro, not only practicing but imparting the secrets he had acquired. All these places are in or near Kyôtô."

"If Ninsei's title to fame rested solely upon the fact that he was the originator of enamelled faience, he would deserve to be remembered. For, though he did not invent these processes, his manner of employing them marked an epoch in the history of his country's Keramics. Under his inspiration the wares of Kyôtô assumed a new character. He was the first to shake himself free from alien influences, whether Chinese or Korean, and to adopt the "natural style" now universally regarded as representative of Japan."

"In Ninsei's hands the faience of Kyôtô became an object of rare beauty. Not only was the *pâte* of his pieces close and hard, but the crackle of the buff or cream-coloured glaze was almost as regular as the meshes of a spider's web. Only the most painstaking manipulation of materials and management of temperature in stoving could have accomplished such results. In later and less conscientious times, the nature of the crackle changed so perceptibly that this one point affords a trustworthy criterion of old and fine ware. Ninsei's crackle was nearly circular. The surface of choice specimens of his handiwork conveys the impression of being covered with very fine netting, rather than with a tracery of intersecting lines. Its appearance is aptly described by the Chinese term " fish-roe crackle." Working, as he did, at different places, varieties are found in the *pâte* of his pieces. The most common is a hard, close-grained clay, verging upon brick-red in colour, and perfectly free from foreign particles. Sometimes the colour changes to a yellowish gray, and the texture becomes nearly as fine as that of pipe-clay. His monochrome glazes are scarcely less remarkable than his crackle. First among them must be placed a metallic black, run over a grass-green in such a way that the latter shows just sufficiently to correct any sombreness of effect. On the surface of this glaze, or else in reserved medallions of cream-like crackle, are painted diapers, and chaste floral designs in gold, silver, red and coloured enamels. Another glaze invented by him, and imitated successfully by the chief experts among his successors, is a pearl-white, through which a pink blush seems to spread. In golden brown, chocolate, and buff he also produced charming tints, and his skill as a modeller was scarcely less than his mastery of mechanical details. As a rule he marked his pieces with the two ideographs *Ninsei* (仁 清) engraved in the paste."

" Genuine specimens of his ware are very scarce. They do exist, and find their way into the market from time to time, but their high value in Japan—as much as two or three hundred dollars are readily paid for a small bowl of the best description—effectually keeps them out of Western collections. If it were required to indicate tests of easy application for determining the claims of a piece attributed to Ninsei, we should name, first the *pâte*, which ought to be very hard and of brick-red or yellowish gray colour; and secondly the crackle, which should be uniform and of circular shape." " Of Ninsei's great contemporary, the painter Tanyu, it can not be denied that he deserved a considerable part of the fame which fell to his lot." " The famous artist and the great Keramist appear to have been fast friends. It is related that they took an equal interest in each other's art, and that many of the pieces manufactured by Ninsei bore designs from the brush of Tanyû or his pupil Yeishin. These designs were largely imitated at the Kyôtô factories, and the popularity of pieces thus decorated was shared by specimens copied from Chinese ware ornamented with fishes from the brush of a Chinese artist, Bokkei, and hence called *Bokkei-bachi*. In fact, public taste turned completely from the sober and severe style of the Seto potters. Decorated faience became the rage, and in some quarters of Kyôtô every second house had its little workshop and kiln."—From BRINKLEY's *History of Japanese Keramics*.

No. 173.—Vase, with globular body and long neck. Height, 9½ in.

> The lower half is unglazed; the upper is covered with skillfully run glazes, russet-brown, black, white, and blue. Mark, *Ninsei*. (Originally in the collection of Kobori Masakadzu, the celebrated *Chajin*.)

No. 174.—Incense-burner, with pierced Lid. Height, 3 in. Diameter, 3 in.

> Decoration, irregular medallions with floral scrolls. Very fine crackle and reddish white glaze. Mark, *Ninsei*.

No. 175.—Cup. Height, 3¾ in. Diameter, 4½ in.

> Decoration, four circular medallions, two containing floral designs and two diapers. The crackle is uniformly round and fine, excellently illustrating a peculiarity of Ninsei's work. Mark, *Ninsei*.

No. 176.—Incense-holder, in the form of a mallard sleeping. Length, 3¼ in. Height, 2 in.

> The feathers are in blue, gold, green, and black. Glaze and crackle of same nature as specimen 174. Mark, *Ninsei*.

No. 177.—Tea Jar. Height, 3 in. Diameter, 2 in.

> Black glaze with an irregular band of white, producing the effect of a silk wrapper. The crackling of the white band is uniformly round. The lower portion is unglazed. Mark, *Ninsei*.

No. 178.—Water-holder, with Lid, barrel-shaped. Height, 8 in. Diameter, 4½ in.

> The body glaze is a greyish buff colour, and over the upper half is run a cream white glaze tinged with red. The clay is left unglazed at the bottom. Mark, *Ninsei*.

AWATA FAIENCE.

"Under Ninsei's influence, however, the industry attained such dimensions that particular kilns began to be spoken of. Among these the most important is that of Awata. It was established about the year 1620 by an artist called Kuzayemon, of whose origin and early history we have no record. At first his productions attracted little attention, but by and by he began to copy Ninsei's methods, decorating his pieces with black and blue pigments, and ultimately with coloured enamels. Ninsei himself visited the Awata factory, and manufactured many good specimens there, although the materials which the district afforded were not of the choicest. The *pâte*, indeed, of the *Awata-yaki* was close, pure, and hard in those early days, but its glaze was not pleasing, being generally of a grayish white, semi-translucent, and lacking the soft yet rich tone which is justly so much admired in fine specimens of Japanese faience. The crackle was uniform and tolerably small, but frequently its too palpable edges imparted to the whole surface a slightly crude aspect. Probably for this reason the Awata potters soon fell into the habit of decorating their pieces more profusely than those of other factories. Early in the eighteenth century, however, a workman whose artist-name was Kinkôzan, effected signal improvements in the Awata ware. Under his treatment the glaze lost its imperfections, and assumed a creamy, lustrous tone, which formed a beautiful ground for the enamels. Among the latter the two principal were grass green and ultramarine. Red was also used, and gold is found almost invariably, its rich sheen harmonizing excellently with the soft buff colour of the glaze. Silver, purple and yellow are rare. Some specimens of *Awata-yaki* are marked with the ideographs *Awa-ta;* others are marked *Kinkô-zan;* but the majority are not thus distinguished. In determining the age of a piece of this faience three rules, equally applicable to all the wares of Kyôtô, may be laid down; first, the *pâte* of choice old specimens is close and hard; secondly, the glaze is lustrous and the crackle fine and uniform; thirdly, the enamels are clear, brilliant, and carefully applied. It may generally be assumed that the degree in which these qualities are present varies directly as the age of a piece, always remembering, however, that when judging Awata faience an exception must be made in respect of specimens manufactured before the time of Kinkôzan (*i.e.*, during the 17th century), for these, while fully satisfying the first and third of the above conditions, usually fail with regard to the second."—From BRINKLEY's *History of Japanese Keramics.*

No. 179—Figure of Daikoku sitting on a Mortar   Height, 9½ in.

    Cleverly modelled. The drapery richly enamelled in gold, blue, and green. Date, 1680.

No. 180.—Incense-burner in the form of figure of Samba (dancer at theatre), kneeling. Height, 9½ in.

    The drapery is in rich blue enamel, with bamboo, pine, and plum decoration in green and gold. Crackling fine and of a circular character. Body glaze, buff coloured. Date, 1690.

No. 181.—Incense-burner in the form of grass-cutter. Female, seated with Basket on her back. Height, 7 in.

    Covered with floral decoration in green, blue, and gold. Crackle of a fine character. Body glaze, a grayish white, by Wanjin, a contemporary of Ninsei.

No. 182.—Incense-burner in the form of Child riding on Hobby horse. Height, 7 in.

    Drapery decorated with various patterns in green, blue, and gold. Crackle, fine and of circular character. Body glaze, buff coloured. Date, 1730.

No. 183.—Figure of the poet H'tomaru, seated. Height, 8 in.

    Drapery richly decorated with green, blue, and gold scrolls, floral medallions and diapers. Crackle fine. Body glaze, buff coloured. Date, 1780.

No. 184.—Figure of Hotei, dancing. Height, 7½ in.

    The upper part of the figure is unglazed, the drapery of the lower part is in red, green, black, and slate-coloured enamels. Date, 1850.

No. 185.—Vase, square in section and tapering below. Height, 8½ in. Side, 3½ in.

    The upper part is pierced in a pattern of intersecting circles, in green and gold. Below, there is a broad band of blue enamel with medallions containing floral subjects. Date, 1780. Body glaze, buff coloured. Mark *Ninsei*.

No. 186.—Vase, square body and spreading base. Height, 8½ in.

    Sides pierced in intersecting circles of gold and blue enamel; the rest of the surface covered with floral scrolls and diapers. Body glaze, buff-coloured. Date, 1800.

No. 187.—Vase, with cylindrical body, tapering below, and spreading neck. Height, 8½ in.

    The body below the shoulder is pierced in a floral scroll, and the part above the shoulder is decorated with horses in gold. Round the lip is a band of chrysanthemums. Body glaze, buff-coloured. Date, 1830.

No. 188.—Wine Bottle, cylindrical with narrow neck. Height, 8½ in. Diameter, 3 in.

    The body is decorated with the seven flowers of autumn, delicately executed in green, red, gold and blue; the space above the shoulder, with a band of medallions containing floral scrolls. Crackle fine and circular. Body glaze, a dark buff. Mark, *Otowa*. Date, 1680.

No. 189.—Censer, hexagonal. Diameter, 5½ in. Height, 3¼ in.

    The upper surface is moulded into the form of a chrysanthemum with petals in blue, brown and gold. The lower halves of the sides are covered with diapers in green, purple, blue, and gold. The upper halves are pierced in archaic patterns. Date, 1820.

No. 190.—Bowl. Diameter, 5½ in. Height, 2¼ in.

> Decorated with figures of Genii in rich enamels, yellow, purple, red, green and blue. Body glaze, a dark buff. Date, 1770.

No. 191.—Cup with narrow base. Height, 3½ in. Diameter, 4¼ in.

> Design, the Genius of the Dragon sitting beside a rock executed in purple, green and black enamels. Body glaze, buff-coloured with reddish mottling in imitation of Korean *Gohon* ware. Mark, *Ninsei*. Made by Dohachi.

No. 192.—Cup. Height, 3 in. Diameter, 4¼ in.

> Covered with a grayish glaze, in which are irregular spots of pink, after the Korean style. Decoration, the mountain Fuji in light blue, with golden clouds and trees in black and blue in the foreground. Mark, *Dohachi*.

No. 193.—Cup. Height, 3½ in. Diameter, 4½ in.

> Covered with a black glaze in which are circular medallions with formal designs in red, green and gold. Mark, *Ninami*. Made by Dohachi.

No. 194.—Cup. Height, 3¼ in. Diameter, 3½ in.

> Covered with a purplish black glaze. The body is encircled by two bands of interlacing medallions with formal diapers in green, purple, yellow, gold and red. Made by Zoroku.

No. 195.—Shallow bowl, irregularly shaped. Diameter, 5¾ in. Height, 2 in.

> Covered with a greyish buff glaze in which are pinkish spots after the Korean style. The outer surface richly decorated with diapers in green, red and gold. Mark, *Sei*. Made by Rokubei.

No. 196.—Cup, round, with flattened sides. Height, 3½ in. Diameter, 5 in.

> Body glaze brown; decoration, roughly executed pines, in blue, gold and white. Mark, *Ninsei*. Made by Rokubei, to imitate Ninsei. (From the collection of Ninagawa Noritane.)

No. 197.—Basket-shaped Vase. Height, 5 in. Diameter, 4 in.

> Covered with a boldly crackled, reddish buff glaze. Mark, *Rokubei*. Made by Rokubei.

No. 198.—Incense-holder, in the form of a Bean-pod. Length, 4 in.

> Body glaze, buff with a red cloud. Decoration, leaves and tendrils in black. Mark, *Sei*. Made by Rokubei.

No. 199.—Figure of Genius, with Gourd. Height, 5½ in.

> Covered with a greenish brown glaze, except the face and one arm, which are unglazed. Mark, *Rokubei*. Made by Rokubei.

No. 200.—Cup. Height, 2 in. Diameter, 1¾ in.

    Decoration, writing (poetry) in red enamel. Mark, *Mokubei*. Made by Mokubei. (From the collection of Ninagawa Noritane.)

No. 200A.—Tea-pot. Height, 4 in. Diameter, 3½ in.

    Thin white porcelain with designs moulded in relief; on the body, dragons and flames; on the lid, waves. Mark (inside lid) *Mokubei*. [Mokubei was the first Japanese Keramist who employed moulds in the manufacture of porcelain.]

No. 201.—Cup. Height, 3½ in. Diameter, 4¾ in.

    Body glaze, buff coloured. Decoration, the seven flowers of autumn, with butterflies Mark, *Ninsei*. Made by Yebissei to imitate Ninsei.

No. 202.—Bowl, square, with rounded corners. Height, 2½ in. Diameter, 5½ in.

    Body, glaze brown; decoration, maple leaves in red, picked out with yellow, and cherry blossoms in white. Mark, *Mokubei*. (From the collection of Ninagawa Noritane.)

No. 203.—Clove-boiler, hexagonal body with tapering neck. Height, 10 in. Diameter, 7 in.

    Completely covered with an elaborate scroll in blue. Date, 1800.

No. 204.—Vase, in shape of elongated Gourd. Height, 9 in.

    Decoration, floral scroll in blue, green and white *engobe*, disposed about white peonies. Mark, *Kinkozan*. Date, 1760.

No. 205.—Vase, with globular body and cylindrical neck. Height, 10½ in.

    Decoration, a diaper of clouds in blue, green and yellow *engobe* with circular medallions containing conventional waves in white *engobe*. Mark, *Kinkozan*. Date, 1760.

No. 206.—Wine Bottle, globular, with thin neck. Height, 9 in. Diameter, 5¼ in.

    The upper portion is decorated with a floral scroll in blue, yellow, and green *engobe* with white peonies. The lower half covered with a buff glaze, having trees, hills, a fan and a hat in blue under the glaze. Date, 1790. This combination of decorations is very rare. Mark, *Hozan*.

No. 207.—Wine Bottle, square, with narrow neck. Height, 9 in. Side, 4½ in.

    Covered with a scroll of leaves and tendrils in blue, green, and yellow *engobe*, disposed about white peonies. Date, 1770.

No. 208.—Clove-boiler in the form of a bag with frilled neck, confined by cord and tassels. Height, 7 in. Diameter, 6 in.

> Covered with scrolls of leaves and tendrils in blue, green, and yellow *engobe*, disposed about white peonies. Date, 1820.

No. 209.—Wine Kettle. Height, 7 in. Diameter, 5½ in.

> Decoration similar to that of No. 208, except that the peonies are replaced by thistle flowers. Date, 1780.

No. 210.—Cup. Diameter, 3½ in. Depth, 2½ in.

> Decoration similar to that of No. 204, the blue enamel being, however, lighter in colour. Date, 1820.

No. 211.—Wine Bottle. Height, 8½ in. Diameter, 5½ in.

> The body is covered with key-pattern diapers in light blue *engobe*, through which wind cords and tassels in red. The neck and shoulders are covered with archaic diapers in green. Date, 1780.

No. 211A.—Vase. Height, 5 in. Lion's heads for handles.

> Decoration same as that of No. 203. Date, 1800.

No. 212.—Wine Bottle, square, with narrow neck. Height, 8 in. Side, 3¾ in.

> Decoration, delicately executed landscapes in blue under the glaze. Body glaze a velvety dark buff. An early specimen of ware made in imitation of Delft faience. Date, 1780.

No. 213.—Vase for washing Wine Cup; narrow base and octagonal body. Height, 4½ in. Diameter, 4½ in.

> Decoration, a number of children at school, trees, etc., in blue under glaze. Body glaze, a velvety cream colour. Same character and period as No. 212.

No. 214.—Wine Bottle, gourd-shaped. Height, 14 in. Diameter, 8 in.

> Body glaze, a lustrous buff colour. Round the base is a broad band of leaf scroll. On opposite sides are two large medallions, with landscapes and floral subject. The rest of the space is covered with dragons and clouds. All the decoration is in blue enamel over the glaze. Mark, *Kacho no fumoto, Hozan* (near Mount Kacho. Made by Hozan).

No. 215.—Wine Vessel, with spout and handle. Height, 7½ in.

> The body covered with a combination of leaf and flower diapers, among which are two circular medallions with landscape and figures. Imitation of Delft faience. Date, 1800.

No. 216.—Oblong Dish. Size, 8¼ in. by 4¼ in.
>Decorated with formal scrolls and medallions in blue and red, to imitate Delft faience. Mark, a *Heron*. Date, 1820.

No. 217.—Bowl. Diameter, 6 in. Depth, 3 in.
>Covered with deep blue glaze, in which are flower and leaf scrolls in white. Date, 1800.

No. 218.—Wine Bottle, square, with narrow neck. Height, 5½ in. Side, 3 in.
>The sides are decorated with landscapes, in blue under the glaze, in panels framed with bands of blue enamel. The shoulders and neck are decorated with alternate bands of blue, green and yellow. Date, 1800.

No. 219.—Incense Box, round. Diameter, 2¾ in. Depth, 1½ in.
>The paste is worked into the semblance of fish's roe. The decoration is in green and blue enamels in relief, subject, storks among clouds and floral scrolls. Date, 1790.

No. 220.—Incense Box, hexagonal. Height, 1½ in. Diameter, 3 in.
>Covered with a raised diaper in green enamel, over which, in high relief, are scrolls of flowers and leaves in blue and gold. Date, 1790.

No. 221.—Incense Box, peach-shaped. Length, 3½ in. Breadth, 2½ in.
>The paste is covered with little holes so as to impart a porous appearance. The design is in relief—a *Howo* and leaves in green, purple and yellow enamels. Stone-ware. Date, 1820.

No. 222.—Incense Burner, hexagonal, with pierced lid. Height, 2 in. Diameter, 3 in.
>Each face contains a floral scroll in high relief on a ground of raised diapers. The faces are unglazed, but between them are bands of blue scrolls on a gold ground. Date, 1810.

No. 223.—Wine Kettle. Height, 6 in. Diameter, 4 in.
>Decoration, panels, containing figure and floral subjects in brown *engobe*, in high relief on an unglazed paste in which a tesselated diaper is impressed. Between the panels and round the spout, base and rim, are bands of blue enamel. Upper surface decorated with floral scrolls in relief. Date, 1840.

No. 224.—Incense Burner, figure of Yebisu riding on Carp. Height, 9½ in. Length, 10 in.
>The fish is red; the face, hands and legs of the god are unglazed; his clothes are in red, yellow, and green enamels with diapers. Date, 1750.

No. 225.—Figure of Hotei and Child, with a Bag which forms a vessel for washing the wine cup. Height, 7½ in. Breadth, 6 in.

> The face, breast, and hands of the god are unglazed; the rest of the piece is decorated with blue and green enamels and gold. Date, 1780.

No. 226.—Clove-boiler. Height, 9 in. Diameter, 6½ in.

> Body glaze, buff coloured. Decoration, plums, bamboos, and pines in green, blue, and gold; on the handle, two half chrysanthemum as crests. Date, 1820.

No. 227.—Incense Burner, with pierced lid. Height, 4½ in. Diameter, 4½ in.

> Decoration, children at play and floral scrolls in red, green, and gold. Date, 1760. (From the collection of Ninagawa Noritane.)

No. 228.—Water Holder, with lid and handles. Height, 3 in. Diameter, 6½ in.

> Body glaze, buff coloured. Decoration, thistle flowers and leaves in red, gold, green, and blue. Date, 1730. (From the collection of Ninagawa Noritane.)

No. 229.—Bowl. Diameter, 7 in. Depth, 3 in.

> Decoration, bunches of thistles in blue, gold, and green, with a band of diapers round the upper edge. Mark, *Awata*. Date, 1780.

No. 230.—Wine Bottle, hexagonal, tapering to the neck.

> Body glaze, buff; decoration, alternate diapers and floral designs, in blue, green, and gold. Date, 1750.

No. 231.—Vase, with body in the form of a ring. Height, 13 in. Diameter, 9 in.

> Body glaze, buff coloured. The front and back surfaces, decorated with medallions, fan-shaped on one side, squares with rounded corners on the other; the former containing floral designs; the latter, figure subjects and floral designs. The sides are covered with diapers. The decoration is in purple, green, blue and gold. Date, 1780.

No. 231A.—Figure of Genius Gama with Toad. Height, 8½ in.

> The breast and face of the Genius are of a dusky brown colour; the toad is a greenish white. The drapery of the figure is a light pink, and the rock on which he stands, green. Date, 1700.

No. 231B.—Two figures, of Goro and Asaina, the latter, attempting to restrain the former, pulls off the skirt of his armour. Height of figures, 10 in. and 15 in., respectively.

> Decorated with blue, yellow, green and gold enamels. Date, 1680.

No. 231C.—Two Cups. The larger, 2½ in. deep; diameter, 4½ in. The smaller, 1¾ in. deep; diameter, 4¾ in.

> The body of the cups is covered with gold and silver on which are medallions with *Tokugawa mon* and scrolls of tendrils. Date, 1800. (These cups formed part of a Shogun's tea equipage.)

No. 231D.—Figure of Hotei and Child, forming an Incense Burner. Height, 4 in. Length, 5 in.

> Head, breast, and arms of god are unglazed; the rest of the group, covered with light gray glaze and sparse floral decoration in black. Date, 1780.

No. 231E.—Flower Vase, square in section with rounded sides and spreading neck. Height, 14 in. Side, 10 in.

> The body is covered with a rich green glaze; the edges, with blue. The decoration consists of *Howo*, floral scrolls, characters, a band of key pattern and figures, all in relief, in a red unglazed clay. The handles are in the form of monsters' heads covered with a deep buff glaze. Date, 1780.

No. 231F.—Figure of Hotei, forming Incense Box.

> Head, back, breast and arms, unglazed; dress covered with an olive-green glaze. Mark, *Tozo*. Date, 1820.

No. 231G.—Cup. Diameter, 4¾ in. Depth, 2½ in.

> Covered with a rich golden brown glaze, except a ring around the bottom, which is white. Made for use in the Shogun's Palace at Yedo. (From the collection of Ninagawa Noritane.) Date, 1840.

No. 231H.—Cup. Diameter, 4½ in. Depth, 2½ in.

> Body glaze, buff coloured with a bold crackle. Decoration, a deep chocolate-coloured band with rushes and conventional waves in blue. Date, 1820. (From the collection of Ninagawa Noritane.)

No. 231K.—Bowl, supported by Three Children. Diameter, 6 in. Depth, 4¼ in.

> Body glaze, reddish brown with inlaid lines and diapers in white clay, after the Korean style. Date, 1800. Mark, *Hozan*.

No. 231L.—Hanging Flower Vase, round. Diameter, 5 in.

> Body glaze, a greenish brown. Design, an old man seated under a tree, a rock, and waterfall, in high relief. Mark, *Hozan*.

(45)

No. 231M.—Incense Burner in form of Japanese Official Cap. Height, 6 in. Length, 9½ in.

>Round the bottom of the sides is a broad band of wood-grain diaper between raised bands of light and dark blue; round the top is a broad band of green, pierced in intersecting circles. Between these bands are delicately executed floral designs in green, blue, and red on a buff ground. The back is covered with a wood-grain diaper in green and blue, the upper surface with a rich green glaze. The top is of silver pierced in a design of bamboos, pines and plums. Date, 1700.

No. 231N.—Tea Jar. Height 3 in. Diameter 2¼ in.

>Decorated with figures of old men and children in green, blue, red, and gold. Date, 1800.

No. 231P.—Incense Burner, globular, with pierced lid. Height, 2½ in. Diameter, 2½ in.

>Round the base a double band of key pattern in blue; the body decorated with chrysanthemums, petals, diapers, and leaves. Date, 1840.

No. 231Q.—Cake Holder, with cover. Diameter, 10 in. Height 10 in.

>Pierced throughout, except at the top and bottom, in a pattern of intersecting circles, and decorated with floral designs in red, blue, green and gold. Date, 1835.

No. 231R.—Cake Holder, with cover. Diameter, 7½ in. Height, 8 in.

>Pierced throughout in a pattern of peony flowers and leaves, and *shishi*. Decorated with red, black, green, blue, and gold. Date, 1840.

FUKAKUSA WARE.

"Although not generally classed among the wares of Kyôtô, the *Fukakusa-yaki* properly belongs to this section. We have already spoken of its originator, Sôshiro, who flourished in the times of the *Taiko* and produced a faience of extremely fine *pâte* decorated with lacquer He worked at Fushimi, a remote suburb of Kyôtô; a place celebrated as the site of the Palace of Pleasure (*Jūraku*), built by Hideyoshi's orders and levelled with the ground after the intrigue of its first inmate, Hidetsugu. The *Fukakusa-yaki* is specially interesting because we find in it the

first figures of faience, or stone-ware, designed for decorative purposes. A worker called Koyemon, who lived at the beginning of the 17th century, has the credit of this innovation, and his pieces attracted so much attention at the time that he received the cognomen of 'Ningiyo-ya' or puppet maker. Since then, the modelling of figures and other quaint subjects has always been a specialty with the Fukakusa artists—a specialty which they supplemented in later years by certain skilful processes designed to give an air of antiquity to their productions. The enamels used in decorating this ware, as well as the fashion of their application sometimes recall the faience of Awata, but the Fukakusa pottery is only partially glazed, while the biscuit is at once harder and darker than that of Kyôtô. After Koyemon the two most celebrated workmen of this factory are Rokuro and Sozaburo, who flourished during the latter half of the seventeenth century. Specimens of the old *Fukakusa-yaki* are among the rarest and most esteemed examples of plastic skill in Japan. They bear no mark, Sôshiro's pieces excepted."
—From BRINKLEY'S *History of Japanese Keramics.*

No. 232.—Fire Holder, cylindrical. Height, 3 in. Diameter, 3¼ in.

    Unglazed pottery with archaic landscapes and trees in black and gold lacquer. Paste a very fine pipeclay. By Soshiro, the first keramist who employed lacquer to decorate pottery. Date, 1595. (From the Ninagawa Collection.)

No. 233.—Figure of Old Man sitting on *Sudzu* (a species of Temple Bell), which he is polishing. Height, 12½ in. Diameter, of *Sudzu*, 7 in.

    The head, legs and hands of the figure are unglazed; the dress is covered with a green paint, the *Sudzu* is gilt. Made by Koyemon, the first keramist who modelled figure subjects for ornamental purposes. Date, 1615.

No. 234.—Incense Burner. Pheasant on Rock. Height, 9 in. Length, 10 in.

    The rock and body of the bird are black; wings, green, red and black; space round eyes white and red. Date, 1780.

No. 235.—Incense Burner, Sparrow-hawk on Rock. Height, 13 in.

    The feathers are slightly glazed in black and white. Date, 1750.

No. 236.—Round Tablet. Diameter, 9 in.

    Design, bird sitting on branch of pine-tree beside a rock; in relief. The bird, tree, and rock, covered with a thin brown glaze. Date, 1780.

KIYOMIZU WARE.

"Otowa-yama is the name of a hill that lies within three-quarters of a mile from the Imperial Palace to the east. On the slope of this hill is the celebrated *Kiyomizu-zaka*, a street which shortly after Ninsei's time became, and has ever since remained, the center of the Keramic industry of Kyôtô."—From BRINKLEY'S *History of Japanese Keramics.*

No. 237.—Cup. Diameter, 5 in. Depth, 3 in.

> Body glaze, a brownish white. Decoration, a band of diapers in green, red and gold. Mark, *Kiyomizu.* Date, 1675. (From the collection of Ninagawa Noritane.)

No. 238.—Incense Box, round. Diameter, 3½ in. Depth, 2 in.

> Body glaze, a very light green; decoration, three pine sprays Mark, *Kiyomizu.* Date, 1680. (From the collection of Ninagawa Noritane.)

No. 239.—Bowl with four small lips. Diameter, 6½ in. Depth, 3 in.

> Body glaze, a grayish white, over which is run, on one side, an irregular patch of dirty green and chocolate brown. Decoration, the seven flowers of autumn. Mark, *Yozo.* Made by Yozo. (From the collection of Ninagawa Noritane.)

No. 240.—Figure of Travelling Priest, seated, with Hat and Bundle, forming Incense Burner. Height, 6 in.

> Body glaze a cream white. Dress, a rich brown glaze of various tones. Date, 1700.

No. 241.—Incense Burner, in form of Lion (*Shishi*) crouching. Length, 8½ in. Height, 5½ in.

> Body glaze, a grayish white; salient lines touched with dark-brown glaze. Date, 1700.

No. 242.—Three Figures of Children, two supporting the third on their hands. Height, 8 in. Breadth, 6 in.

> Body glaze, a grayish white. Hair of children touched with black. Date, 1800.

No. 243.—Figure of Devil raising Lantern. Height, 11 in.

> Unglazed. Date, 1820.

No. 244.—Figure of Hotei, with Bag, forming Incense Burner. Height, 2 in. Width, 4 in.

    Hotei's face and breast are unglazed ; his bag and dress are covered with a green glaze flecked with blue. Date, 1800.

No. 245.—Dish, with indented edges. Diameter, 5½ in.

    Body glaze. cream-coloured with very large crackle. Decoration, conventional forms in black and blue. Date, 1840. (From the collection of Ninagawa Noritane.)

No 245A.—Pagoda, forming Incense Burner. Height, 11 in. Side of base, 5½ in.

    The roof and basement stones coloured dark brown. the sides veined to imitate wood. Very delicate workmanship. Mark, *Kahei* (maker's name). Date, 1800.

No. 245B.—Tea-pot. Height, 4 in. Diameter, 3½ in.

    Very fine pipe-clay, unglazed. The decoration consists of a cock on a drum, flowers, characters, &c., in red, gold and white and pink *engobe*. Mark (under handle) *Rantei* (name of maker). In seal character beside the handle is the name *Joun* (name of painter). In gold, on the left of the handle :—*Shogetsuzan Rantei seizo* (made by Rantei Shogetsuzan). Date, 1840. (From the Ninagawa collection.)

IWAKURA WARE.

" It is recorded that Ninsei's pupils were numerous, but tradition has paid him the silent tribute of consigning their names, for the most part, to oblivion. We hear of them only through their works. One of them established a factory at Iwakura, in the suburbs of Kyôtô, and, receiving there the instruction and assistance of his master, produced pieces faithful in all details to Ninsei's style. These manufactures were generally marked with the two ideographs *Iwa-kura*, in an oval (*vide* Plates of Kyôtô Marks). With regard to the nature of the early Iwakura ware, there is not much difficulty in distinguishing it from that of Awata. The *pâte* of the former was finer and lighter in colour than that of the latter, and, the composition of the glazes being virtually the same in both cases, this superiority of *pâte* imparted to the *Iwakura-yaki* a fuller and warmer tone. Perhaps the difference may be best described by saying that the body-colour of the Iwakura faience was a light buff ; that of the Awata, a bluish white. The methods of decoration were identical, except that the style of the potters of Awata was somewhat florid, while that of the Iwakura artists was chaste even to severity. The reason of this dissimilarity is doubtless to be found in the Iwakura ware's superior beauty of surface, which forbade a too profuse application of enamels and pigments. In such a matter, however, the fashion of course varied with the time. Thus, at the end of the seventeenth century, Tsunayoshi, fifth Shogun of the Tokugawa dynasty, evinced an exceptional taste for ware ornamented with designs in gold, and accordingly we find that the works of that era were particularly rich and ornate. The artists did not escape Court influences, and specimens of their productions during and subsequent to that period deserve to be classed with the finest examples of Japanese enamelled faience."—From BRINKLEY's *History of Japanese Keramics*.

No. 246.—Cake Box, with lid. Height, 6½ in. Diameter, 5 in.

    Divided by spiral lines of gold into eight spaces filled with diapers in rich enamels (green and blue), among which are medallions containing conventional birds and chrysanthemums. Date, 1720. Mark, *Iwakura*. (From the collection of Ninagawa Noritane.) (This shape and design has been extensively copied of recent years, but the execution and enamels of the modern pieces are altogether inferior.)

No. 247.—Cake Box. Height, 4 in. Diameter, 4½ in.

    Made with a double shell; the inner solid, the outer pierced in various diapers. Cream coloured without decoration. Date, 1780.

No. 248.—Cup. Depth, 2¾ in. Diameter, 4¼.

    Body glaze, dead-leaf colour. Decoration, radishes and leaves in light brown and black. Mark, *Iwakura*. Date, 1760.

No. 249.—Bowl in shape of blossom of *Kikiyo*.

    Body glaze, a grayish white. Decorated outside with blossoms of carnation, light blue under the glaze; inside, with pear-shaped lines in brown with metallic spots. Date, 1800. (From the collection of Ninagawa Noritane.)

No. 250.—Cup. Diameter, 4½ in. Depth, 2½ in.

    Body glaze, cream color, with three Tokugawa *mon* in black. Date, 1830. (From the collection of Ninagawa Noritane.)

No. 251.—Cup. Same size as No. 250.

    Body glaze, buff. Decoration. a straw rope, with leaves, &c., attached. Date, 1840. (From the collection of Ninagawa Noritane.)

No. 252.—Cup. Diameter, 3¾ in. Depth, 2 in.
> Body glaze, a brownish white. No decoration. A hard paste, almost stoneware. Date, 1680. From the collection of Ninagawa Noritane.)

No. 253.—Hanging Flower Vase in form of Mask of Demon. Size, 7 in. x 7 in.
> Body glaze, grayish white, with fine well-marked crackle. Horns, hair and teeth covered with a golden brown glaze. Date, 1750.

No. 254.—Tea Jar. Height, 7 in. Diameter, 5 in.
> Upper part covered with black glaze, on which are delicately executed diapers of waves and clouds, and dragons coiled in the form of ellipses, supporting alternately *Kiku* and *Kiri* (Imperial crests). Date, 1860. Black Wood Top inlaid with Silver.

MIZORO WARE, CALLED ALSO GOBOSATSU.

"Another pupil of Ninsei, by name Gensuke, established a factory in the suburbs of Kyôtô, at a place called Mizoro, or Gobosatsu The signification of the word "Mizoro" is honorable (*Mi*) muddy (*zo*) lake (*ro*); from which it will be understood that the site of Gensuke's workshop was chosen with reference to properties which the clay of this marshy district was supposed to possess. They were not very excellent properties, for the *Mizoro-yaki* is distinguished from the wares of Iwakura and Awata by the greater density and coarseness of its *pâte* and the larger crackle of its glaze. The decoration was at first very simple. The designs, which generally consisted of miniature pines or tufts of broad-bladed grass, were executed in black, chocolate-brown, or dark blue. Subsequently, however, we find pieces ornamented in the *reservé* style : monochrome enamel (always grass-green) is applied to the whole surface with the exception of the parts that carry the pictorial designs." " Genuine specimens are exceedingly rare, as the manufacture was soon discontinued."—From BRINKLEY's *History of Japanese Keramics*.

No. 255.—Wine Bottle, globular, with narrow neck. Height, 8 in. Diameter, 5 in.
> Covered with a clear green glaze on which are maple leaves in red, blue, gold, and purple, with a black trellis. The neck is a creamy white, with bands of gold, blue, red, and green diapers. Date, 1750. Mark, *Gobosatsu*.

No. 256.—Pair of Wine Bottles, rectangular in section, with narrow neck and rounded shoulders below.

> Body glaze, a grayish white. On the broad faces are floral decorations in yellow, blue, and white *engobe;* on the narrow faces characters signifying different species of wine (*Nindo* and *Awamori*). The necks are decorated with leaf scrolls in black and white, *engobe,* and the shoulders with representations of drapery. Date, 1760.

No. 257.—Incense Box in the form of Chrysanthemum, with pierced lid. Diameter, 3 in. Depth, 1½.

> Body glaze, a brownish white, with a band of scroll-work and black lines. Date, 1780. Mark, *Gobosatsu.*

No. 258.—Cup. Diameter, 4½ in. Depth, 2½ in.

> Covered outside with an iron-red glaze, speckled; inside with a greenish brown. Date, 1800. Mark, *Gobosatsu.*

EIRAKU WARE.

'The processes which Mokubei had originated were extended and perfected by Zengoro-Hozen, commonly called Eiraku." "This man's specialty was the manufacture of urns (*furo*) for the *Chajin*. His factory was at Nara, and he enjoyed the patronage of the renowned dilettanti Shukô and Jô-ô. After his death (1558), his son, Nishimura Sôzen, moved to Sakai, in Senshû; and Sôzen's son, of the same name, transferred his residence, in 1594, to Shimo-kyô-roku-jô, in Kyôtô, from whence one more move to Anraku-kôji brought the family to the house it occupied until nearly the middle of the present century." "The representative of the eleventh generation was Zengoro-Hozen. At first, content to follow the route trodden by his ancestors, he confined himself to the production of unglazed urns for the use of the Tea Clubs. Even in this work the remarkable dexterity with which he blended *pâtes* of different colours gave earnest of greater achievements in other branches of the Keramic art. This promise was soon fulfilled. Practising porcelain manufacture as a species of pastime in the intervals of his regular trade, he ultimately developed such skill that his celadons and pieces decorated with blue under the glaze attracted wide attention. To these he soon added admirable imitations of the old Cochin-Chinese faiences. The conditions of the time were especially favourable. Long continued peace had filled the coffers of the nobles and induced those luxurious habits of life among which art products find their best market. The Court at Yedo, presided over by Iyenari, eleventh Prince of the Tokugawa dynasty, set an example of brilliant extravagance to which the feudal princes were nothing loath to conform, while the now well-established custom of sending to the Shogun yearly presents of pottery and porcelain from the various districts, had engendered a wholesome rivalry among the provincial factories. Before long Zengoro's fame attracted the attention of Harunori, Lord of Kishû. He invited the potter (A. D. 1827) to his province, and there set up for him, within the precincts of the Castle Park, a kiln at which was produced the celebrated *Oniwa-yaki*, or *Kairaku* ware as it is also called from the stamp it bears. It was an imitation of the Cochin-Chinese faience described above, but in purity of colour it scarcely equalled its original. Like Luca della Robbia, Zengoro made the composition and application of glazes an especial study. We search the works of his successors and predecessors in vain for examples of parallel perfection in this branch of Keramics. His Aubergine porcelain, and the rich combinations of turquoise blue, purple, and yellow shown in the glazes of his faience, amply justify the immense popularity attained by the Kairaku ware. A prominent place among his achievements belongs to his "*Kinrande*" or "*Akaji-kinga*," which bears the stamp "*Eraku*." The idea of this porcelain was derived from the much-valued Chinese "rouge vif" of the *Yung-lo* period (1403-25), and the Japanese potter succeeded in producing a colour little inferior to that of the original. In fact his coral-red glaze, lustrous and at the same time exquisitely soft, with its wealth of golden decoration and reserved medallions in brilliant cobalt, must be classed among the Keramic master-pieces not of Japan alone but of the whole world. These terms, *Kinrande* (scarlet-and-gold-brocade pattern) and *Akaji-kinga* (golden designs on a red ground), are descriptive. The stamp *Eiraku* was suggested by the Japanese pronunciation of the Chinese period-name *Yung-lo*. The Chief of Kishû also bestowed upon Zengoro another seal inscribed with the ideographs *Ka hin Shi-riu* (*vide* Plates of Kyoto Marks). This seal, Zengoro appears to have used to mark his choicest pieces only; a distinction which accords with the material of which the two seals were made, that bearing the characters *Eiraku* being of silver, and that bearing the characters *Kahin-Shiriu* of gold. From the time of his visit to Kishû the potter's fame rapidly augmented. It became the fashion with the magnates of the Western capital to give him orders, and their amusement to test his skill by asking him to copy *chefs-d'œuvre* of Chinese, Korean, and even Dutch manufacture which had been handed down in their families for generations. Zengoro's success in these trials of skill is said to have been remarkable. It is recorded that a tea-urn, secretly borrowed by a Court Noble called Takatsukasa from the custodians of the Kono-e heirlooms, was so perfectly imitated at the Eiraku workshop that the original and the imitation were not distinguishable. This feat procured for Zengoro another seal bearing the inscription *Tôkin-ken* (the weighty potter); a mark which is not found upon his wares. From Prince Arisugawa he also received a document conferring the title of *Itô-seimei* (the world-renowned Keramist). Opulent and respected, Zengoro might now have passed the remainder of his days in repose and comfort. But his heart was in his art. Like Bernard Palissy, the successful production of a new glaze was to him almost a matter of life and death. He had mastered the processes required to produce the purple, yellow, turquoise, and green faience of Cochin China, the blue-and-white, coral-red, and enamelled porcelains of China. Two things only he could not copy: the stanniferous glaze of the Delft faience and the transmutation glazes of the Po-yang Lake. To the investigation of these he applied himself diligently, gradually spending upon fruitless experiments the money he had accumulated by his previous works."—From BRINKLEY's *History of Japanese Keramics*.

No. 259.—Incense Box, round. Diameter, 4¼ in.

    Covered with gold leaf; the lid has a chrysanthemum in white chalk in high relief. Made by Nishimura Sozen, ancestor of Zengoro Hozen (Eiraku). Date, 1640. (From the collection of Ninagawa Noritane).

No. 260.—Bowl. Diameter, 5 in. Depth, 2½ in.

    Covered with a coral-red glaze. On the outside are three medallions with the Imperial *kiri* crest in rich gold, the intervening spaces covered with bamboos, pines, and plums, also in gold. Under the rim, inside, is a band of diapers, and on the bottom, the character *Fuku* (prosperity), surrounded with a formal scroll, all in gold. The space between these two bands is occupied by 7 characters in rich blue (*Zen niyo no Kura o gon ari*) being a verse from the Sutras. Mark, *Kahin Shiriu*. This bowl was probably made for presentation to the Emperor. Rich Gold Lacquer Stand,

No. 261.—Wine Bottle in shape of Pomegranate. Height, 5 in. Diameter, 5 in.

    Covered with a coral-red glaze on which are floral scrolls and *Howo* in gold. Mark, *Dai Nipon Eiraku sei* (Made by Eiraku, Dai Nipon). Lip cased in silver.

No. 262.—Octagonal Bowl with narrow base. Diameter, 7½ in. Depth, 4½ in.

>On the outside, an elephant, a lion, a unicorn, and a kirin: over their backs in circles of flame are the characters *yei* (everlasting), *ki* (honorable), *cho* (long), and *ho* (to endure). The intervening spaces are filled with archaic designs. Round the inside is a floral scroll, and on the bottom a *Howo*. The decoration is entirely in gold. Mark, *Kutani ni oite Eiraku Sei* (Made by Eiraku at Kutani), in black on a blue ground.

No. 263.—Bowl, round. Diameter, 6½ in. Depth, 3½ in.

>Coral-red glaze, with dragon, phenix, flames, flowers, and archaic symbols in gold. Mark, *Kutani ni oite Eiraku Sei* (Made by Eiraku at Kutani). On the bottom, inside, a blue scroll, with the character *Fuku* (prosperity), in the centre.

No. 264.—Fire Holder. Diameter, 4½ in. Depth, 2½ in.

>Coral-red glaze, decorated outside with plums, pines, and bamboos in gold, among which are four reserved circular medallions with the characters *Mi-yo Manzai* (may your honorable dynasty last ten thousand years), in deep blue. Round the rim, inside, a band of birds and floral designs. Mark, *Dai Nipon Eiraku Sei* (Made by Eiraku, Dai Nipon). Date, 1835.

No. 265.—Bowl. Diameter, 8¼ in. Depth, 3½ in.

>Coral-red, covered inside and outside with floral scrolls in gold. On the bottom the character *Fuku* (prosperity) in gold on a gold ground, round which is a band of white with a scroll of dragons in gold. This piece is by Zengoro Tokuzen, son of the celebrated Zengoro Hozen. It is marked, *Dai Nipon Eiraku-Sei*. (Made by Eiraku, Dai Nipon.) Date, 1840.

No. 266.—Nest of Two Cups, with Saucer. Diameter of cups, 2¼ in. and 2½ in. respectively. Depth, 1¼ in. Diameter of saucer, 4½ in.

>Coral-red glaze. The under surface of the saucer has a floral scroll in gold; the upper, fishes, conventional waves, and diapers. The cups are similarly decorated inside; their outsides have medallions with *Howo* and floral scrolls. Each piece is marked *Dai Nipon Eiraku-Sei* (Made by Eiraku, Dai Nipon.) These are by the same maker as No. 265.

No. 267—Fire Holder, circular with three legs. Diameter, 8½ in. Height, 6 in.

>Covered inside and outside with a rich green glaze, on which are various forms of the Imperial crest in relief, in yellow, blue, brown, white, purple, and golden brown. Mark, *Eiraku*. By Zengoro Hozen.

No. 268.—Fire Holder, hexagonal, with rounded sides and legs. Diameter, 10 in. Height, 8½ in.

>Same glaze and decoration as No. 267; the green colour, however, is a little lighter. The lid is purple and pierced in a design of *Kiri* leaves. Mark, *Eiraku*. By Zengoro Hozen.

No. 269.—Bowl, with Cover. Diameter, 6½ in. Height, 5½ in.

>Covered with a rich green glaze. On the outside are *Howo* and flames in relief, in yellow, blue, purple and white. On the inside, incised flowers. Mark, *Eiraku*. By Zengoro Hozen.

No. 270.—Bowl, with spreading neck and narrow base. Height, 6 in. Diameter, 7 in.

>The base is a rich purple; the body, yellow with archaic mountains and pines in relief. The inside is covered with gold leaf. Mark, *Eiraku*. By Zengoro Hozen.

No. 271.—Bowl, with Pedestal. Height, 5 in. Diameter, 7 in.

>Covered inside and outside with a rich purple glaze. Mark, *Eiraku*. By Zengoro Hozen.

No. 272.—Tea Jar, with Metal Lid. Height, 6 in. Diameter, 5 in.

>Body glaze, purple with chrysanthemums and leaf scrolls in yellow and green in relief. Round the shoulder are four loops standing in a band of green, with plum blossoms in yellow. Mark, *Eiraku*. By Zengoro Hozen.

No. 273.—Incense Box, square. Side, 2 in. Depth, 1½ in.

>The edges and bottom covered with rich purple glaze, the sides with green, on which are floral designs in yellow in relief; the top, with a rich golden brown having archaic designs in relief. Mark, *Eiraku*. By Zengoro Hozen.

No. 274.—Cup. Diameter, 3¾ in.

>Covered with a rich ivory-white glaze. On the outside are *Howo* and archaic designs in slight relief. Mark, *Kahin Shiriu*. Made by Zengoro Hozen. Gold Lacquer Stand.

No. 275.—Wine Cup. Diameter, 2¼ in. Depth, 1¼ in.

>Same character as No. 274, except that the design is inside and in bolder relief. Mark, *Eiraku*. By Zengoro Hozen.

No. 276.—Wine Cup. Diameter, 3½ in. Depth, 1¼ in.

>Same in every respect as No. 275, except that the colour of the glaze is not so warm. Same mark and maker as No. 275.

No. 277.—Tea Jar. Height, 3½ in. Diameter, 2½ in.

>White, with floral scroll in high relief. Mark, *Dai Nihon Eiraku Sei* (Made by Eiraku, Dai Nihon). Made by Zengoro Tokuzen.

No. 278.—Wine Bottle. Height, 4½ in. Diameter, 3½ in.

    Ribbed horizontally; the edges of the ribs being green, the hollows golden brown. The bottom and inside are covered with green glaze. Mark, *Eiraku*. Made by Zengoro Hozen.

No. 279.—Fire Holder, with pierced Lid. Height, 3½ in. Diameter, 5¼ in.

    Made of two species of very fine clay, one black, the other a light red. The clays run into one another so as to present a marbled appearance. Unglazed. Mark, *Hozen*. Made by Eiraku Hozen.

No. 280.—Vase, cylindrical, with swelling body. Height, 7½ in. Diameter, 2½ in.

    Same in every respect as No. 279, except that three incised diapers stretch down from the neck.

No. 281.—Circular Cake Box, with Lid. Height, 2½ in. Diameter, 5 in.

    Porcelain, decorated with blue and white under the glaze. Design, five-clawed dragons, flowers, and children at play. Mark, *Eiraku Hozen Konan ni seisu*. (Made by Eiraku Hozen on the south of the lake—*i. e.*, Lake Biwa.)

No. 282.—Incense Box, circular, with conical Lid. Height, 2½ in. Diameter, 2½ in.

    Porcelain, decorated with blue under the glaze. Design, pine, plum, and bamboo. Mark, *Eiraku*.

No. 283.—Cup. Diameter, 4½ in. Depth, 2½ in.

    Covered with a light green glaze, having encaustic designs in white clay after the Korean style. Mark, *Eiraku*. Made by Eiraku Hozen. (From the collection of Ninagawa Noritane.)

No. 284.—Wine Cup. Diameter, 2 in. Depth, 1¼ in.

    Faience, decorated with blue under the glaze. Design, medallions with landscape and figure subjects, the intervening space filled in with plums, pines, and bamboos. Mark, *Dai Nipon Eiraku sei*. (Made by Eiraku, Dai Nipon.)

MISCELLANEOUS.

"Another great name among the Kyôtô Keramists is that of Dôhachi Takahashi, a contemporary of Zengoro Hôzen. He commenced his career at a workshop in Gojô-zaka (Kyôtô) about the year 1825. He was a potter of considerable technical skill in the manufacture of his glazes, one of which, a peculiar dull white with a tinge of pink, is almost equal to Ninsei's work from which it was copied. The designs on his faience also exhibit some of the most graceful conceptions of the truly Japanese school. In the year 1830, his reputation had become so well established that we find him employed as an instructor by the potters of Takamatsu, in Sanshû, and Himeji, in Banshû. It is curious, however, to observe that even at this late period of the art's history alien influences are still perceptible. Prior to the enforced immigration of Korean workmen, the *Taiko* had attempted to achieve a mutual engrafting of the two countries' styles by importing, as models for the Keramists of Japan, a quantity of Korean faience. The chief characteristic, and indeed the only redeeming feature, of the latter—which was called *Gohon* or "Pattern-ware"—consisted in light pink tints or flecks in the glaze, and these we often find exactly reproduced in Dohachi's best pieces, side by side with designs not unworthy of Tanyû's brush. Strange that after the lapse of two cycles and a half, the "plebeian prince's" conception should have been so perfectly realized by one of his country's most æsthetic artisans! In his old age Dôhachi took the name of Ninami, with which also he marked some of his pieces. In general, however, he used the ideographs *Dô-hachi* for this purpose."—From BRINKLEY's *History of Japanese Keramics*.

No. 285.—Wine Cup. Diameter, 2¼ in. Depth, 1¼ in.
    Porcelain. Base and rim encircled by bands of key pattern and scrolls in blue under the glaze. The rest of the outer surface decorated with delicately executed medallions containing figure subjects, and with diapers in red over the glaze. Mark, *Dohachi*.

No. 286.—Scent Bottle, gourd-shaped. Height, 2 in. Diameter, 1¼ in.
    Decortaion, diapers in white on a blue ground. By Dohachi.

No. 287.—Netsuke. Diameter, 1½ in.
    Upper surface decorated with diapers in white on a blue ground; lower, with bamboos in blue on a white ground. Probably by Dohachi.

No. 288.—Tea Pot. Height, 4½ in. Diameter, 3 in.
> White porcelain decorated with figure subjects in green, blue, red, and purple enamels. By Shuhei.

No. 289.—Tea Jar. Height, 3 in. Diameter, 2½ in.
> White porcelain decorated with blue under the glaze. Round the neck a band of drapery; round the base a band of diapers with the characters *Dai Nipon Toko Shuhei Kore wotsukuru*. (Made by the potter Shuhei of Dai Niphon). (From the collection of Ninagawa Noritane.)

No. 290.—Wine Cup. Diameter, 2¼ in. Depth, 1¾ in.
> Porcelain. On the bottom, inside, is a peony, and round the base, outside, a band of key pattern in blue under the glaze. The rest of the outer surface is covered with a blood-red glaze, and floral designs in gold. Mark, *Shuhei Sei*. (Made by Shuhei.) (From the collection of Ninagawa Noritane.)

No. 291.—Square Tea Jar. Side, 2¾ in. Depth, 3 in.
> Faience. Covered with canary-yellow glaze; floral scrolls in brown and black under the glaze. Imitation of Dutch polychromatic ware. Date, 1800. (This species of decoration is very rare.)

AKAHADA WARE.

"This ware derives its name from a barren hill called Akahada, which overlooks the little town of Gojo in Yamato. The district is one of peculiar Keramic interest, for it includes the village of Haji, where clay substitutes for human sacrifices were first made, nineteen hundred years ago, at the suggestion of Nomi no Sukune, the prince of wrestlers. The kiln at Akahada is said to be of considerable antiquity, but, however this may be, it was only under Nomura Ninsei's direction that its productions began to exhibit any merit. The *pâte* of the early pieces (1630-1650) shows a greater admixture of sand than that of the contemporary Kyôtô faience—for which in other respects it might easily be mistaken—while the glaze is opaque and of a grayish tint with black speckles. Red has always been a predominant colour in the decoration, which, for the rest, follows Ninsei's style, though some pieces exhibit all the severity of the ancient school. The old *Akahada-yaki* is in all probability little known to foreign collectors, for the manufacture was discontinued about 1650, and not revived until the beginning of the present century, when it again became a flourishing production under the auspices of Yanagi-sawa, lord of Koriyama, a "Chajin" of considerable note, who is said to have painted some of the pieces himself. Among the productions of the second period is a very beautiful variety, in which the surface is covered with a dull layer of gold, while the decoration consists of floral designs or diapers, sometimes in white slip, but more generally traced with a paste formed of glue and the white powder called "Shiroi." Commoner varieties of this second-period ware are a faience with a light-buff *pâte* and a grayish white glaze, decorated with colours and gilding, and a stone-ware covered with dark-green or olive-brown glaze, and having impressed designs. The Akahada ware is generally marked with some form of the ideographs *Aka-hada*."—From BRINKLEY'S *History of Japanese Keramics*.

No. 292.—Cup. Diameter, 4¼ in. Height, 3½ in.

> Faience. Covered with a finely crackled buff glaze. Decoration, a circular medallion of red enamel resting on a green leaf, tipped with yellow. In the medallion is a figure of Hotei in gold, red, and green. On the right of the medallion are the characters *Mokuhaku utsusu* (copied by Mokuhaku) with his seal in red. On the left, *Koriyama Riuri-kiyo tsutsushinde Yempuku-hitsu ni yegaku* (Painted by Riuri-kiyo of Koriyama in the hall called Yempuku). Mark, *Akahada*, and impressed characters *Mokuhaku*. Date, 1820.

No. 293.—Flower Vase, with tapering base and broad shoulder. Height, 11 in. Diameter, 5 in.

> Faience. Covered with a *flambé* glaze brown and white. Mark, *Akahada*. Date, 1780.

No. 294.—Water Holder, with spreading neck and handles in form of Craw Fish. Height, 6 in. Diameter, 5½ in.

> Faience. Body glaze, buff, crackled Decoration, round the base, a band of green and blue diaper; the rest of the body covered with red diapers, among which are reserved medallions with landscapes and floral subjects. The lid is covered with a rich brown glaze. Mark, *Akahada* and *Mokuhaku*. Date, 1830.

No. 295.—Basket-shaped Cake Holder. Diameter, 6 in. Height, 5½ in.

> Covered with gold leaf, on which are chrysanthemums in white and green in relief. Mark, *Akahada-yama*. Date, 1840.

KENZAN WARE (FAIENCE)

"The history of the Keramics of Kyôtô is a record of individuals, not of factories. Ninsei's figure overshadows all the rest, and next to him, at no great distance in some respects, comes Ogata Sansei, commonly called Kenzan. Ogata was born at Narutaki-mura, in the suburbs of Kyôtô, in the year 1660; that is to say, just at the time when the methods introduced by Ninsei and Wanjin had fairly won their way to public favour. He was the second son of Ogata Sôken, and his younger brother was the celebrated painter Kôrin. Sansei, who appears to have been called also Shinsei and Shinsaburo, was himself a painter of considerable promise, but his proclivities fortunately lay in the direction of Keramics. After he had studied literature and poesy under the well-remembered Hirosawa Nagayoshi, and the mysteries of the *Cha no Yu* under Zuiriu Sôsa, whom the men of the next generation elevated into a semi-divinity under the title of Nichiren Sôsa, he spent a short time in the practice of his father's favorite art, and his pictures are said to have given earnest of great talent. That he preferred to devote his brush to the ornamentation of faience was partly, perhaps, because the designs furnished for that purpose by Tanyu and Yeishin had attracted so much attention, and partly because his brother Kôrin, in whom he must have recognized a greater artist than himself, had already developed a taste for lacquer decoration. At first he appears to have applied himself diligently to the study of technical processes, taking for his instructors the potters of Raku, Seto, and Zeze. Very soon, however, he developed an original style, of which the chief characteristics are great boldness, combined with a very skilful disposition of tints both in the execution of designs and in surface decoration. Kenzan is, in fact, a perfect representative of the genuine Japanese school, which requires that results, however elaborate, shall convey no idea of detailed effort, and enforces strict obedience to the natural principle of limited impressions. A branch of plum blossoms, a tuft of feathery reeds and bending grasses, a family of sparrows clustering amid the foliage of a bamboo, or the blue crest of a mountain peeping through a haze of golden clouds—such things as these can be comprehended at a single glance, and are, therefore, legitimate subjects for representation in the circumscribed field which the artist has at his disposal. Kenzan thoroughly understood this. His designs are often exceedingly artistic for all their simplicity, and the landscapes depicted on some of his smaller pieces embody most graceful conceptions. He preferred *Shibu-ye* and *Ai-ye*—designs in black, russet-brown and blue—to *Kin-ye*—designs in coloured enamels and gold. But in all three varieties of decoration he showed himself equally a master. His best pieces were potted at Awata, and neither their *pâte* nor their glaze is distinguishable from that of the ordinary *Awata-yaki*. The style, however, can not possibly be mistaken. A further guide is the cachet: Kenzan marked all his pieces with his name, *Kenzan* (乾山). Sometimes he used clay from other localities, especially that from Shigaraki (*vide Shigaraki-yaki*), which produced a coarse, gritty *pâte*, far inferior to the *Awata-yaki*, but well adapted to the exceptionally bold outline-sketches which, with true artistic instinct, he invariably employed in the ornamentation of these rougher specimens. At a late period of his career we find him working at Iriya, in Yedo (now Tôkyô), but the materials procurable in the neighbourhood of the Eastern capital were of such inferior quality that even Kenzan could produce nothing satisfactory with them. Urged rather by love for his craft than desire of gain, he never attempted to manufacture large quantities of faience, so that genuine specimens of his work are exceedingly rare and proportionately valued. His style was, however, copied with tolerable fidelity and success by his son and grandson, whose pieces, marked with the same cachet, Kenzan, only differ from those of Ogata himself in being slightly inferior both in technique and artistic qualities."—From BRINKLEY'S *History of Japanese Keramics*.

No. 296.—Jar, with Lid. Height, 8 in. Diameter, 7½ in.

    Decoration, leaves boldly executed in red, white, green, black, blue, and yellow. Mark, *Kenzan*. This piece was formerly in the possession of Kobori Masakazu, the celebrated *Cha-jin*.

No. 297.—Incense Box of irregular shape. Length, 3½ in. Breadth, 3 in. Depth, 3¾ in.

    The top is decorated with a landscape and figure subjects in gold, brown, green and blue. The sides are covered with diapers in black. The inside is decorated with black and gold. Mark, *Kenzan*.

No. 298.—Incense Box, round. Diameter, 4 in.

    Decoration, bands of formal scrolls and diapers in black. Mark, *Kenzan*.

No. 299.—Large Plate. Diameter, 18 in.

    Covered with a grayish white glaze. Decoration, a bold design of trees and leaves in brown and green. Mark, *Kenzan*. Made by the grandson of the first *Kenzan*.

No. 299A.—Figure of Otafuku, the Japanese Venus. Height, 8 in.

    Face and hands unglazed; hair black; drapery decorated with maple leaves in yellow, green, and red, and diapers in black. (From the collection of Ninagawa Noritane.)

RAKU WARE (FAIENCE).

"About the year 1525, a Korean potter, known as Ame-ya, came and settled in Japan. It is doubtful whether the man's proper name was Ame-ya, or whether he came from a part of Korea thus called. At any rate, before he had long resided in Japan, he changed his name to Masakichi, and married a Japanese woman called Teirin. Masakichi had probably hoped to find in Japan a profitable field for the exercise of his calling. But the times, and also—a candid critic would be disposed to say—his own homely methods, were against him. He set up a kiln in Kyôtô, and began to turn out a sort of archæic faience, which went by the appellation of *So-kei-yaki*, Sokei being the industrial name taken by Masakichi. The ware did not attract much attention until after Masakichi's death, when his wife, who seems to have been a woman of considerable taste, took the kiln into her own hands. Sen-no Rikiu was then beginning to rank as a master of the *Cha no Yu*. He discovered in this *Ama-yaki*—as Teirin's ware was called—something that pleased his æsthetic instincts, and to signify his approval he bestowed upon the son of its neat-fingered manufacturess his own surname, Tanaka, which he had just exchanged for that of Rikiu. After his mother's decease this son, whose *prénom* was Chojiro, continued to produce the same faience in a street called Kamichôja-machi, Kyôtô. Even Sen-no Rikiu's patronage did not at first bring the ware into favour. But in the year 1518, the Regent Nobunaga, at Rikiu's inspiration, gave Chojiro a large order for cups and other tea utensils, with the immediate result of making the *Amayaki* fashionable. Ten years afterwards, Hideyoshi summoned Chojiro to his palace of Juraku, and was so pleased with his productions that he presented to him a gold seal bearing the ideograph *Raku*, which from that time became at once the name and mark of a ware exceedingly popular with the Japanese Tea Clubs. Chojiro died in 1592, just as the order to bring from Korea a number of his father's countrymen and fellow-experts was on the point of being carried into effect.

" The *Raku-yaki* of those times was a hand-made pottery, with scarcely any technical excellence, and only one artistic recommendation, viz., quaintness of shape. But the clay used in its manufacture possessed non-conductive properties, which rendered it peculiarly suitable for tea-drinking purposes. Western amateurs have difficulty in reaching an æsthetic platform high enough to appreciate the almost impertinent simplicity of this faience, and certainly there was nothing admirable in its dull black glaze, a most defective imitation of the rich and glossy Chinese *Temmoku* (*Kien-yô*). The glazing material was obtained by powdering the gravel of the River Kamo—a somewhat refractory material, it would seem, for the choicest specimens of the ware possess anything but an uniform surface. Another variety, which dates from Chojiro's time, was covered with a light red or salmon-coloured glaze, produced by the action of heat on a clay originally yellow, and consequently presenting a patchy, crude appearance, the reverse of beautiful. Nevertheless, during six generations, extending over a period of more than a century and a half, the *Raku* potters achieved nothing beyond these two glazes. Considerable dexterity they did, indeed, display, not only in adapting the shapes of their pieces to the tastes of Tea Clubs, but sometimes also in moulding them after a fashion that would not disgrace an artist of our own days. This is especially true of Doniu, Choyu's grandson. He is popularly known as Nonko, and has been placed at the head of his school by common verdict. But it is not till the time of Choniu (1759) that we find any pieces of *Raku* ware at all likely to conciliate Western taste. That artist added a tolerably rich, though dull, green glaze to those handed down by his predecessors; succeeded, also, in producing variegated glaze, and, further, employed gold for decorative purposes, so that in the eyes of European connoisseurs he may justly be esteemed the real originator of the *Raku-yaki*. After his time we find pieces not altogether devoid of attraction, such as, for example, vases or incense-burners of a grass green faience, having reticulated devices picked out with gold. But, on the whole, this *Raku-yaki* is essentially the ware of the Tea Clubs, and most of the specimens which have found their way westward were either made expressly for foreign markets or purchased as curiosities rather than as ornaments. It may probably be said with truth of the *Raku-yaki* that its representative specimens are the most *rococo* of all Japanese faiences. The chief object of the *Raku* potters appears to have been to produce a rustic vessel entirely free from any qualities calculated to divert attention to itself rather than to its uses."—From BRINKLEY's *History of Japanese Keramics*.

No. 300.—Cup. Diameter, 5 in. Depth, 3 in.

    Black glaze, veined with red. Date, 1700.

No. 301.—Incense Box, square. Side, 2¼ in. Depth, 1½ in.

    Covered with a deeply incised scroll pattern. Glaze, brownish white. Mark (on inside of lid) *Raku*. Made by *Doniu*, commonly called *Nonko*.

No. 302.—Medicine Box, round. Diameter, 2¼ in.

    Black glaze with incised diapers, and dragon, waves, lion, pine tree and flowers in relief. Date, 1780.

No. 303.—Fire Box, square. Side, 9½ in. Depth, 7½ in.

> Covered inside with a tea-coloured glaze; outside, partially covered with a black glaze, partially unglazed. Decorated with shells of various sorts in red, green, yellow, white, and blue enamels. Date, 1790.

No. 304.—Cake Box, in the form of the god Hotei, seated on a bag of corn. Height, 5½ in. Diameter of bag, 5½ in.

> The bag is covered with a white glaze, crackled. The breast, face, arms and legs of the god, and an ear of corn which protrudes from the bag, are unglazed. The dress of the god is green, his fan brown, black and purple. Mark, *Seiniu* (ninth descendant of Sokei).

No. 305.—Chess Board and Box of Chessmen. Height of Board, 7 in. Sides, 14 in. and 12 in.

> The top of the board has a design of two water wheels and flower blossoms scattered over the surface in blue under the glaze. On the sides are archaic designs and diapers in green, red, and blue. The box containing the chessmen has on the top a circle of storks in blue among conventional clouds in red. On the sides are diapers in blue and red. The chessmen are made of Kutani porcelain. Date of board, 1780; of men, 1720.

KUTANI WARE.

"After the wares of Hizen, Kyôtô, and Satsuma, there is none better known, outside Japan, than the *Kutani-yaki*. The origin of the factory is attributed to Mayeda Toshiharu, lord of Taichoji, in the province of Kaga, who caused a kiln to be built at the village of Kutani, and placed it under the direction of his vassal, Tamura Gonzayemon. The exact date of this event is not known, but it certainly lies between the years 1635 and 1660. It does not appear that any Keramic industry had existed in Kaga before that time—a condition which probably resulted from the comparatively isolated position of the province, lying as it does on the extreme west of Japan, and being separated by a lofty range of mountains from Kyôtô, the centre of luxury and art-patronage. The productions of the new kiln were after the fashion of the old Seto ware; that is to say, tea-jars and water-vessels of dark clay covered with a light chocolate glaze. In 1665, however, Toshiharu's son, Toshiaki, anxious to develop the so-far unpromising enterprise which his father had inaugurated, sent one Goto Saijiro to Hizen, for the purpose of acquiring the methods of porcelain manufacture. On his return the nature of the *Kutani-yaki* underwent a complete change."

" Yet there is nothing at all perplexing or doubtful about the history of the Kutani factories. During the seventeenth and early part of the eighteenth century, the wares produced there were of two sorts. The first, and more characteristic, was the *Ao-Kutani*, so called from a deep-green (*ao*) glaze, of great brilliancy and beauty, which was largely used in its decoration. Associated with this glaze were others, not less lustrous and full-toned—yellow, purple, and sometimes a soft Prussian blue. These glazes were laid on so as to form diapers, scrolls, and floral designs; or they were simply run over designs traced in black on the biscuit. Thus the decoration must be regarded as, and was indeed confessed to be, an imitation of that attributed to the potters of Cochin China in their *Kôchi-yaki*. The second class of ware was decorated somewhat after the Arita fashion, with this principal difference—that the Kutani potters never, so far as we know, employed blue under the glaze in conjunction with enamels. Their chief colours were green and red, supplemented by purple, yellow, blue (enamel), and gold. Red was a specialty. They produced a peculiarly soft, subdued, full-bodied colour, varying from a rich Indian-red to a russet-brown. For designs, the early potters had recourse to a well-known artist, Kuzumi Morikage, of the Kano school, who loved to depict miniature landscapes, flowers ruffled by the breeze, sparrows perched among plum-branches, and other glimpses of nature in her simplest garb. We never find anything resembling that wealth of brilliant blossoms and massing of bold colours by which the porcelain of Arita was distinguished. The Keramists of Kaga were always faithful to the fashions inaugurated by Morikage. On many of their best productions the decoration is of a purely formal character—diapers, scrolls, and medallions containing conventional symbols. The only figure-subjects met with are the Chinese *Karako*, or children at play. As with the faience of Satsuma, so with the ware of Kutani, the amateur may be quite sure that specimens decorated with peacocks, groups of chrysanthemums and peonies, figures of wrinkled saints or brightly draped ladies, cocks upon drums, and so forth, belong to the manufactures of modern times."

" So far we have spoken of the style of decoration only. The *pâte* remains to be considered. Here a difficulty presents itself. The potters of Kutani originally took their clay from a hill near the village of Azayatsu. It was not porcelain earth: it was not even capable of being manufactured into good pottery. Thus we find that some of the oldest pieces of this ware are technically very faulty. But these pieces do not belong to either of the classes mentioned above. The incongruity of applying lustrous glazes or rich enamels to a radically defective *pâte* was recognized at once, and the Kutani artists, baffled by the refactory nature of their local materials, imported good clay from Hizen or any other convenient place. Sometimes they used this imported clay only; sometimes they eked it out by an admixture of earth procurable on the spot; sometimes they even went so far as to apply their own decorative processes and marks to biscuit manufactured elsewhere. There resulted a considerable source of perplexity for the amateur. Among specimens of the old *Ao-Kutani* he will find stone-ware and porcelain; while, on the other hand, pieces decorated after the fashions inaugurated by Kuzumi Morikage are, with very rare exceptions, excellent porcelain. We have seen pieces of *Kutani-yaki*, dating as far back as the beginning of the eighteenth century, which would bear comparison with the best Hizen egg-shell. It has to be confessed, therefore, that among all the wares of Japan the *Kutani-yaki* alone offers a *pâte* as likely to mislead as to instruct. This is especially true of blue-and-white specimens. We have said that, so far as we know or have been able to ascertain from Japanese experts, *bleue sous couverte* is never found upon old Kutani ware in conjunction with enamelled decoration. But pieces decorated with blue only, though rare, are occasionally met with. In these the connoisseur's only guides will generally be the nature of the glaze and the tone of the blue. The latter lacks the depth and richness of the best Hizen blues, and is equally removed from the delicate purity of the Hirado colour. It is, in fact, an inferior, somewhat impure pigment. This, however, is obviously an uncertain criterion. The glaze is more trustworthy. It shows a peculiar waxy softness which generally suffices to establish a distinction. But, in truth, specimens of blue-and-white Kutani are so very exceptional that we need scarcely dwell upon their characteristics. In the case of polychrome pieces, the richness and lustre of the enamels, their full clear colours, and the severity of the decorative style constitute features easily identifiable. Above all, the beauty of the glaze is incomparable. In choice specimens, its tone almost equals that of the celebrated ivory-white of China."—From BRINKLEY'S *History of Japanese Keramics*.

No. 306.—Dish, with Pedestal. Diameter, 12½ in. Depth, 3¾ in.

Stone-ware. The pedestal is covered with a yellow glaze, having archaic waves and pine trees in black. The rest of the surface is covered with a rich green glaze, under which are leaf and floral diapers and a *Howo* in black. Date, 1680.

No. 307.—Plate. Diameter, 13½ in.

Stone-ware. The bottom is covered with a yellow glaze, over which are a diaper of petals and a gourd with leaves and tendrils in rich green and blue. Round the inner rim is a deep band of rich green with diapers in dark blue. The outside is covered with a yellow glaze, having leaf scrolls in black. Mark, *Fuku*, in seal character. Date, 1660. (From the collection of Ninagawa Noritane.)

No. 308.—Plate. Diameter, 8½ in.

> Stone-ware. Upper surface covered with a green glaze, in which are diapers in dark blue disposed round a flower and leaves in purple and yellow. On the rim are two strips of purple and yellow. The outside is yellow with black scroll. Mark, *Fuku* in seal character. Date, 1700.

No. 309.—Dish. Diameter, 17½ in. Depth, 3½ in.

> Porcelain. Covered inside and outside with a light green glaze, in which is a scroll of tendrils in yellow with chrysanthemums in blue. Date, 1820.

No. 310.—Dish. Diameter, 15½ in. Depth, 3½ in.

> Porcelain. A cream white glaze, the inner surface elaborately decorated with three *gumbai* (war-fans) and bunches of flowers and leaves in rich green, blue, yellow, and purple enamels. Round the outside a leaf scroll. Mark, *Fuku* in seal character. Date, 1830.

No. 311.—Dish. Diameter, 15 in. Depth, 4 in.

> Stone-ware. Round the edge of the inner surface is a broad band of diapers in panels, in yellow, blue, purple, and green enamels. Below this are two bands of key pattern, one green, the other blue. The bottom is covered with a yellow glaze, having for design a purple lobster with blue eyes, entangled in a black net. The outside is covered with a green glaze, having black scrolls of tendrils. Mark, *Fuku* in seal character. Date, 1820.

No. 312.—Water-Holder. Diameter, 12 in. Depth, 8¾ in.

> Stone-ware. The outer surface is covered with a green glaze, among which are two purple dragons with conventional clouds in blue, yellow, gold, and white. Round the inner edge is a wide band of scroll pattern in blue. Inside are fishes in purple, green and yellow. Mark, *Kutani* in a yellow square. Date, 1820.

No. 313.—Wine Bottle, gourd shaped. Height, 8½ in. Diameter, 4 in.

> Porcelain. Covered with a green glaze, under which are diapers in black. Date, 1830.

No. 314.—Wine bottle, gourd shaped, hexagonal in section. Height, 9 in. Diameter, 3½ in.

> Faience. The faces of the lower lobe are covered with yellow and green enamels in blue-edged panels with black diapers. Round the shoulder is a broad band of yellow diaper with circular medallions, reserved, containing archaic designs in blue, green, and purple. The neck is decorated with leaves and scrolls in similar colors. Mark, *Fuku* in seal character. Date, 1820.

No. 315.—Bowl. Diameter, 5½ in. Depth, 2¼ in.

>Porcelain. Covered with yellow glaze, on which are leaves and flowers in green and purple. Mark, *Kutani Kichizo*, in seal character. Date, 1830.

No. 316.—Wine Bottle, hexagonal with rounded shoulders. Height, 6½ in. Diameter, 3 in.

>Stone-ware. Covered with a yellow glaze, on which are leaves and flowers in purple, green, and blue. Mark, *Fuku*, in seal character. Date, 1820. (From the collection of Ninagawa Noritane.)

No. 317.—Incense Burner, square. Side, 2 in. Height, 2 in.

>Porcelain. Covered with a rich green glaze and black diapers. On each face is a reserved medallion, circular, with floral designs in red, yellow, green and purple. Date, 1820. (From the collection of Ninagawa Noritane.)

No. 318.—Incense Burner, square with high feet. Height, 2¾ in. Side, 2¼ in.

>Porcelain. Covered with a fine diaper in green and red, in which are reserved medallions with figure subjects in green, red, yellow, and purple. Date, 1820.

No. 319.—Incense Burner, square. Side, 3 in. Height, 3¼ in.

>Porcelain. Covered with a diaper of russet red: on the sides are reserved medallions, containing floral subjects, a bird on a bough, etc., in green, yellow, blue, and purple enamels. Date, 1710. Silver top.

No. 320.—Incense Box, in the shape of a sleeping duck. Length, 3 in. Breadth, 2 in.

>Stone-ware. Covered with yellow, blue, and green enamels. Date, 1830.

No. 321.—Bowl, round with scalloped edge. Diameter, 6¼ in. Depth, 2½ in.

>Porcelain. Covered with elaborate and delicately executed diapers and medallions in green, purple, and yellow. Mark, *Fuku*, in seal character. Date, 1750.

No. 322.—Incense Box, in form of Sparrow. Length, 3 in. Breadth, 2¾ in.

>Porcelain. The lower half is covered with blue enamel on which are floral designs in yellow, green, and purple; the feathers of the bird are in russet red. Date, 1830.

No. 323.—Incense Burner, with pierced Lid and Handles. Height, 2½ in. Diameter, 3 in.

> Covered with delicately executed diapers in red, gold, and green, among which are medallions in gold with floral scrolls. Date, 1700.

No. 324.—Wine Bottle, hexagonal in section with rounded base and neck. Height, 5½ in. Diameter, 2¼ in.

> Porcelain. The shoulders have medallions containing coiled dragons in light red on a red ground with floral scrolls in gold. The body is covered with diapers in green and yellow. Round the base is a scroll of blue. Mark, *Shoreido, Kichizo Seisu* (Made by Kichizo at the kiln Shoreido), and seal of Tozan. Date, 1830.

No. 325.—Incense Box, cylindrical. Height, 2 in. Diameter, 2½ in.

> Porcelain. Body decorated with irregular bands of red diapers, between which are bamboos and pines in green and purple. On the top are rocks and plum blossoms in red, purple, blue, and green. Date, 1740.

No. 326.—Tea Pot. Height, 2 in. Diameter, 1¼ in.

> Porcelain. On the sides and lid are medallions with delicately executed figure subjects and landscapes in green, blue, gold and red. The rest of the surface is covered with a red glaze on which are diapers in gold. Mark, on bottom and at base of handle, *Kutani*. Date, 1835.

No. 327.—Bowl. Diameter, 6 in. Depth, 3 in.

> Egg-shell porcelain. Round the outside are three circular medallions in red with floral designs in gold. The rest of the outer surface and half of the inner are decorated with the *Yorakude* design (cords and tassels). Date, 1700. N.B.—Egg-shell Kutani ware is seldom to be found.

No. 328.—Bowl, ribbed. Diameter, 6 in. Depth, 2½ in.

> Porcelain. Decorated inside with maple and fern leaves entangled in a fine meshed net. Outside, scrolls of vine leaves and tendrils running vertically. These designs are in red, green, blue, and gold. Date, 1750.

No. 329.—Bowl. Diameter, 6 in. Depth, 1¾ in.

> Porcelain. Inside, fishes in red and gold caught in a fine meshed net. Outside, diapers in red, blue, yellow, and green. Mark, *Sei* (quiet or silent), in seal character. Date, 1830.

No. 330.—Plates, diamond-shaped. Five. Length, 6 in. Breadth, 4½ in.

> Porcelain. Inner surface decorated with two patches of diaper in red, blue, and purple, between which is a tree squirrel in red among green, blue, and yellow leaves and branches. Mark, *Fuku*, in seal character (blue under the glaze). Date 1700.

No. 331.—Incense Box, peach-shaped. Length, 2¼ in. Breadth, 1½ in.

> Porcelain. Design, a jay sitting on a branch. Painted by Kudzumi Morikage. Date, 1680.

No. 332.—Cake Box. Diameter, 8½ in. Depth, 6 in.

> Stone-ware. Covered with diapers in red, picked out with purple, green, and yellow, among which are medallions containing floral subjects, birds and children at play, in green, purple, yellow, and blue. Date, 1750.

No. 333.—Vase, gourd-shaped. Height, 11 in. Diameter, 6½ in.

> Porcelain. On the bottom lobe, among blue scrolls, are large medallions with landscapes in green, yellow, blue, and purple. The upper lobe is richly decorated in panels and bands of variously coloured diapers, leaf scrolls. &c. Mark, *Fuku*, in seal character. Date, 1820.

No. 334.—Jar, with Lid. Height, 10 in. Diameter, 5 in.

> On the sides, large panels with rock and flowers; between the panels scrolls of vine-leaves and tendrils. Round the neck and base are bands of leaves and diapers in red. The colours of the body decoration are green, blue, purple, and red. Date, 1710.

No. 335.—Bottle. Height, 9½ in. Diameter, 5½ in.

> Round the neck are bands of black, red, yellow, and blue. Below these is a broad band of diapers vertically divided by waving lines of green, yellow, and black. The body is decorated with flowers growing above a trellis work. Date, 1700.

No. 336.—Bottle, with swelling body and narrow neck. Height, 10 in. Diameter, 5½ in.

> Round the neck and the upper and lower portions of the body are deep bands of red. The rest of the body is divided in vertical strips containing alternately diapers in red and chains in green through which pass lines of yellow globules. Date, 1680.

No. 337.—Plate, octagonal. Diameter, 9 in.

> Decorated outside with a floral scroll in blue and purple. On the upper surface, within a broad band of scalloped diaper in green and yellow, is a water scene with geese and reeds, in green, blue, purple, and red. Date, 1700. Mark, *Fuku*, in a blue square.

No. 338.—Bowls, with Lids, two. Diameter, 4¼ in. Height, 3½ in.

> Round the base of each bowl and the top of the lid is a delicately executed band of scroll pattern and chrysanthemums. The rest of the outer surface is covered with red in which is a scroll of flowers and tendrils in gold. The inside, of cup and lid, is covered with delicately executed bands of diapers and archaic designs in red, yellow, blue, green, and gold. These bowls are from the factory of Hachiroyemon. Mark, *Fuku*.

No. 339.—Bowl, with Lid. Diameter, 5½ in. Height, 3 in.

    The decoration consists of medallions containing diapers in red, surrounded by blue borders of archaic design. The space between the medallions is covered with red on which is a scroll pattern in gold. This bowl is also by Hachiroyemon, but it differs from No. 338 in being made of clay procured at Kutani, whereas the former contains a large admixture of Hizen clay. Date, 1820.

No. 340.—Incense Box, square. Side, 2 in. Depth, 1 in.

    Porcelain. The sides are covered with blue, green and yellow enamels, having scroll patterns and diapers in black. The top has a yellow glaze with a landscape under it delicately pencilled in black. The inside of the lid is glazed yellow and has the name of the maker (*Yoshitoshi*) reserved. On the bottom, inside and outside, are the maker's seals, and mark of the period *Bunsei* (1818–29) in a blue circle.

No. 341.—Incense Box, round. Diameter, 2½ in. Depth, 1 in.

    Faience. The body is covered, inside, with a white glaze, crackled; outside with a rich green glaze having diapers in black. The top is decorated outside with a floral scroll in blue, yellow, and purple enamels, surrounded by a blue border. On the lid inside is the character *Fuku*. Date, 1820.

No 342.—Tea Jar. Height, 3 in. Diameter, 3 in.

    Faience. Body glaze, ivory white, crackled. The top, shoulders and base are decorated with bands of diaper, leaves, floral scrolls, &c, in blue, green, red, and gold. The body is divided by gold lines into three panels containing delicately executed landscapes in blue, green, red, and gold. Date, 1860.

IMBE, OR BIZEN (STONE-WARE).

"The *Imbe* ware was produced at a place of the same name in the province of Bizen. Pottery was no doubt made in this district at a very early date, but does not seem to have attracted any attention before the end of the fifth century. Even then, too, it was of the coarsest description, its gritty red *pâte* and unglazed surface fitting it for the manufacture of only the commonest utensils. From Hideyoshi's time (1580) a considerable improvement became visible. The clay was manipulated with greater care, and some of the specimens are compared by connoisseurs to the Chinese boccaro, which they were no doubt intended to imitate. The most valued pieces of this *Kok-Bizen* (old Bizen) are those stamped with the shape of a new moon (*Mika-zuki*), a waning moon (*Kayezuki*), or the characters "*Kokubei;*" while another slightly inferior variety bears the delineation of a cherry-blossom. Originally the terms *Bizen-yaki* and *Imbe-yaki* were interchangeable; but by degrees the former came to be applied to the unglazed, the latter to the glazed specimens; while a third term, *Hidasuki*, was introduced to describe a variety in which the surface is marbled by irregular patches or lines of red. A tolerable idea of the pottery's qualifications, as well as of the Tea Clubs' proclivities, may be formed from the fact that this marbled effect is obtained by tying straw ropes round the piece before placing it in the oven, and that an approved specimen of the rough unglazed result—which resembles nothing more than a half-baked brick—easily finds a purchaser to-day at from fifty to one hundred dollars."

"This criticism applies only to the Bizen pottery of old times. Towards the close of the seventeenth century the character of the ware underwent marked improvement. A slate-coloured or a brown *pâte*, fine as pipe-clay and almost as hard as porcelain, was used to model figures of deities, genii, birds, fishes, and mythical animals. It is scarcely possible to speak in too high terms of the plastic ability thenceforth developed by the Bizen potters. Their best efforts are admirably faithful, and will bear comparison with similar work produced in any country and at any age. A little later they used a red clay giving a *pâte* scarcely less fine and hard than that of the *Ao-Bizen*, as the former variety is called. The glaze applied to this red *pâte* is peculiar to Bizen. Its colour and metallic sheen give it exactly the appearance of the beautiful *Sentoku*, or golden bronze. Those who have seen choice specimens of this middle-period Bizen stone-ware cannot hesitate to class it among the very highest achievements of Japanese art. As for the Bizen pottery of our own time, we need only say that it has shared the general degeneracy of its fellows. The red-clay figures of obese deities and unreal monsters that, now-a-days, stand in every *bric-a-brac* shop, may possess some attraction borrowed from the traditions they recall, but cannot be counted types of either cunning craft or praiseworthy art."—From BRINKLEY's *History of Japanese Keramics.*

No. 343.—Incense Burner, in the shape of a Peony growing from a rock, with two *shishi* playing on the top. Height, 8 in. Width of base, 7 in.

Greenish gray *pâte*, unglazed. Exceedingly delicate workmanship. Date. 1700.

No. 344.—Incense Burner, in the shape of a Boat with Fisherman sitting in the bow. Length, 12½ in. Height, 5¼ in.

Same *pâte* and period as No. 343.

No. 345.—Incense Burner, archaic shape with perforated sides and Silver Top. Height, 4½ in. Width, 5½ in.

A hard, reddish, stone-ware, the surface covered with impressed diapers. Date, 1660.

No. 346.—Incense Burner, in the form of a Cat sitting on Fire Box covered with a bamboo blind. Height, 6½ in. Width, 4 in.

A reddish stone-ware covered with brown, speckled glaze. Date, 1750.

No. 347.—Incense Burner, in the form of a Cock perched on a Roof. Height, 12 in. Roof, 8 in. by 6 in.

Brown stone-ware covered with a golden gray glaze. Date, 1800.

No. 348.—Hanging Vase, in the form of a Shell. Length, 8¼ in.

Covered with a reddish brown glaze. Mark, *Kichi* (name of maker). Date, 1780.

No. 349.—Vase, in the form of a Basket. Height, 6¼ in. Diameter, 7 in.

A greenish gray *pâte*. Date, 1700.

No. 350.—Incense Burner, in the form of *Shishi*. Height, 3 in. Width, 3½ in.

Red clay and glaze. Date, 1770.

No. 351.—Paper Weight, in the form of a Lion crouching. Height, 2 in. Length, 2 in.

A greenish gray clay. Date, 1780.

No. 351A.—Incense Burner, in the form of an Ox standing on a Corn-stack. Height, 5½ in.

Red stone-ware. Date, 1730.

No. 351B.—Figure of Yebisu, with Carp. Height, 7½ in.

Red stone-ware. Date, 1800.

HIGO WARE (CALLED ALSO YATSUSHIRO OR UDO WARE). (FAIENCE.)

"The principal province of Kiushiu is Higo, which lies to the south of Hizen. The feudal chief of this province, at the end of the sixteenth century, was the renowned warrior Kato Kiyomasa, who led the expedition of 1592 to Korea. Returning in 1598, he brought with him a Korean potter who had previously exercised his trade at Pusan. This man's name was Sonkai (Japanese pronunciation), but on being enrolled among the vassals of Kato Kiyomasa he became Uyeno Kizo. Keramic factories had existed in Higo for six centuries before Sonkai's arrival, but their productions were limited to coarse household utensils. The principal of them was at a place called Tôda, near the flourishing sea-port town of Yatsushiro. Opposite to the latter lies the large island of Amakusa, long renowned for the excellence of its potter's earth (*vide Kameyama-yaki*). Sonkai, or Kizo, settled at Tôda, and, using one of the clays of Amakusa, which gave a fine, iron-red *pâte*, produced a faience called at first *Tôda-yaki*, and subsequently *Yatsushiro-yaki*. It is one of the most delicate and æsthetic of all Japanese faiences. The *pâte*, as has been said, is of exceedingly fine texture, and its red colour, combining with the pearl-gray of the diaphanous glaze—which in the older pieces is uniform, lustrous, and minutely crackled—produces a tint of great richness. The decoration generally consists of storks flying among clouds, or of simple combinations of lines and diapers. It is peculiar in the fact that the designs are engraved in the *pâte* and afterwards filled with white clay before glazing. It is, in short, a copy of the Korean pottery known in Japan as *Unkaku* (clouds and storks), to which, though slightly inferior in point of glaze, it is decidedly superior in delicacy and beauty of finish. But, on the other hand, neither the *Yatsushiro-yaki*, nor its Korean progenitor, can by any means bear comparison with the Chinese faience which is the original of both. Another very favourite variety of this ware imitates the Korean *Hakime*, or 'streaked' pottery, in which the white engraved design is intended to represent the marks (*me*) of a coarse brush (*haki*), the intention being to convey an idea of boldness and rapidity of finish. The potters of Yatsushiro confined themselves almost entirely to this inlaid decoration. They never used enamels or pigments of any sort. Their wares, therefore, require little description, the universal characteristics being a fine, iron-red or dark gray *pâte*, a tolerably lustrous glaze varying from pearl-gray to dark brown, and white inlaid decoration, the clay of the latter showing crackle of greater or less fineness.

Sonkai having been enrolled among the vassals of the Chief of Higo, his family received a perpetual pension. After his death his second son, Uyeno Chôbei —his eldest son had remained in Korea—and his third son, Uyeno Tôshiro, carried on the manufacture at separate kilns. The names of the successive representatives of the family do not deserve individual mention, until the time of Uyeno Shûzo, seventh in descent from Chôbei, who distinguished himself by the beauty of his workmanship. The branch of the family founded by the third son, Tôshiro, also divided into two; Tôshiro's eldest son, Torosuke, establishing a *bekke*, or independent house, as is frequently done in Japan. Sixth in descent from this Torosuke, that is to say, in the eighth generation of the Sonkai family, we find a workman called Uyeno Gentaro, who appears to have been the first of the Higo potters to mark his pieces. He employed the initial ideograph (*Gen*) of his name. The direct line of the Uyeno Toshiro branch was continued in the person of his second son, seventh in descent, from whom came a skilful workman, Uyeno Yahachiro. It will thus be seen that the manufacture of the *Yatsushiro-yaki* was carried on by three families of experts, and tradition says that the products of the three factories were equally excellent. There appears, at all events, to have been no attempt made by any of the three to depart from their original models. The *Yatsushiro-yaki* is remarkably uniform in character. The glaze is always the same translucid brown, varying only in degree of darkness, and prevaded sometimes by a bluish, sometimes by a greenish tinge; and the *pâte* shows little difference from generation to generation, except that it is harder and finer in specimens of early manufacture. Occasionally we find imitations of the polychrome Satsuma glazes—as olive-green or brown flecked with blue and white—but these are rare exceptions.

About the year 1780, a tentative effort was made to produce porcelain at Amitayama, in the Udo district of Higo. Considerable success was achieved, but the factory, failing to obtain sufficient patronage, was closed in a short time. Specimens of this ware are exceedingly rare, and unless they are marked, the amateur can not hope to distinguish them from Hirado porcelain."—From BRINKLEY'S *History of Japanese Keramics*.

No. 352.—Shallow Bowl. Diameter, 12 in. Depth, 3½ in.

    Covered with a brown glaze. The inner surface has inlaid designs in white clay, and the outer wavy bands. Made to imitate Korean ware. Date, 1610.

No. 353.—Plate, with elevated base. Diameter, 7¼ in.

    Ware and decoration similar to No. 352. This piece has been baked in an inverted position. The decoration of the under surface is richer than that of the upper. Date, 1610.

(76)

No. 354.—Bowl. Diameter, 7½ in. Depth, 3 in.

    Body glaze, a dark brown. The inside and outside have inlaid designs in white clay to imitate the marks of a brush. Copied from the Korean ware known as *Hakime Mishima*. Date, 1630.

No. 355.—Incense Burner, cylindrical. Height, 3 in. Diameter, 2½ in.

    Covered with a greenish brown glaze, and having a flight of conventional storks among clouds in white round the body. Imitation of Korean *Unkaku* ware. Date, 1650.

No. 356.—Deep Cup. Height, 3¾ in. Diameter, 3½ in.

    The body glaze is a bluish brown : the decoration inlaid, consisting of archaic designs in white and black. Date, 1620.

No. 357.—Tea Jar. Height, 3 in. Diameter, 3 in.

    The upper part of the body is covered with an olive green glaze; the neck is flecked with white and blue. A glaze precisely similar to this was produced at the Satsuma factory in its early days. Date, 1620.

No. 358.—Bon-bon Holder, in form of Jar with lid. Height, 3½ in. Diameter, 3½ in.

    The body glaze, a dark brown; the decoration, inlaid, consisting of floral scrolls in white clay. Date, 1780. Mark, *Gen* (name of maker).

No. 359.—Incense Box. Diameter, 2¼ in. Depth, 1¼ in.

    The body glaze, a dark brown. On the top a cherry-blossom in white. Mark, *Sai* (name of maker). Date, 1800.

No. 360.—Vegetable Bowls, two. Cylindrical, indented so that the section is a figure of eight. Height, 3 in. Section, 3¼ in. x 2 in.

    The body glaze, brown flecked with blue. The decoration is inlaid, and consists of sheaves of rice in white clay. Mark, a cross. Date, 1820.

BANKO WARE (FAIENCE).

'At the village of Kuwana, in the province of Ise, between the years 1760 and 1795, there lived a rich merchant, by name Kuwanami Gozayemon, who in the days of his prosperity turned his thoughts to garden-making, that refined extravagance which has always been among the first fancies of a wealthy Japanese. Until that time Gozayemon had given himself little concern about the 'Chajin' and their tenets, but his horticultural predilections necessarily drove him to seek the aid of those masters of æsthetics. To this end he visited Kyôtô, and there became the pupil of a renowned *virtuoso*, from whom he acquired, not the principles of garden-making alone, but also that taste for Keramics which forms an integral part of the Tea Ceremonials. The memory of the great potter Kenzan was then fresh, and the Kiyomizu factories had attained the zenith of their excellence. The merchant of Kuwana, now an ardent disciple of the *Cha-no-Yu* ethics, never wearied of wandering from workshop to workshop and watching the clay assume, under the touch of skilled manipulators, shapes the beauties of which he had newly learned to appreciate. His interest gradually developed into a desire to imitate. The Kyôtô potters were easily persuaded to explain their processes, and whether their pupil possessed some innate ability, or whether, as a wealthy amateur, he was able to command the best materials and devote ample time to the manufacture of single pieces, it is certain that, by the circle of friends who were so fortunate as to receive the products of his kiln, he was pronounced one of the best artists of his day. Yet, like the majority of Japanese Keramists, he was an imitator, not an originator. The thick, unadorned Raku ware, and the ill-favored Korean faiences supplied models that seemed not less worthy of reproduction than the delicate conceptions of Ninsei or the bold designs of Kenzan. In both directions, however, Gozayemon was eminently successful; so successful that his fame reached the Court at Yedo, and a special order was sent to him from the Shogun Iyenari (1785). No doubt such a commission incited the amateur to more than common exertions, for the proficiency he displayed induced the Shogun to summon him to Yedo. He accordingly moved to Komme, in the north-east suburb of the Eastern Capital, where he already possessed a residence, and there pursued his Keramic pastime under the patronage of the Court nobles, Iyenari himself sometimes condescending to visit Komme and watch the elaboration of results which he so much admired. The effect of all this upon Gozayemon's reputation can be easily conceived. His ware became the rage everywhere—not, perhaps, for the sake of its merits alone, but also because of the difficulty men experienced in procuring it; for fame had made the artist capricious, and, since he did not work for gain, none but the favored few might obtain specimens of his handicraft. **He** now no longer restricted himself to imitations of the ancient models, but, giving the reins to his fancy, turned out pieces which combined the graces of the Japanese school with the brilliancy of the Chinese polychromatic porcelain. Just then, however, the factories of the Celestial Kingdom, under the munificent patronage of the Emperor Chien-lung, were producing wares not unworthy of their ancient fame ; and, side by side with these, the inferiority of the Japanese Keramist's enamels became easily apparent. The Shogun, therefore, commissioned the Governor of Nagasaki to procure from King-te-chang the recipes used at the Imperial factory, together with a supply of the best materials. One is a little puzzled to conceive by what means these instructions were carried out, but the Governor seems to have experienced no difficulty, for within a year he forwarded to Yedo all that was required. With this aid, Gozayemon's success was more marked than ever. The best connoisseurs could scarcely distinguish his pieces from the Chinese porcelain decorated with red and green enamels of the Wan-lieh period (1673–1620), though indeed it must be confessed that the models he copied do not exhibit any very remarkable degree of Keramic skill. His imitations of the Delft faience, too, were certainly quite as good as the very inferior specimens of that ware which found their way to Japan ; but of his achievements in this line we need only say that they would not be admitted into any respectable European collection. He only became great when, departing from his models, he combined brilliantly glazed surfaces with chaste floral decoration in the pure Japanese style. He imitated everything, from the rude faiences of Korea and the grand colors of Cochin-China to the severest styles of Ninsei and Kenzan. He generally marked his pieces *Banko* (everlasting or enduring), sometimes, however, adding *Fuyeki* (changeless). His productions are now known as *Ko-Banko-yaki* (old *Banko* ware). He died about the year 1800, at Kuwana, whither he had been recalled by Matsu-daira, lord of Etchiu, one of the most celebrated of modern *virtuosi*. Whatever talent he possessed died with him, for, since he cultivated Keramics entirely as a pastime, he neither took pupils nor imparted his art to his children. One of his relatives, by name Takekawa Chikusai, who resided at Izawa, in Ise, made some attempts to continue the manufacture, or, rather, sought to obtain a market for his own wares under the ægis of the *Banko* stamp. But his productions were only tolerable so long as the materials left by Gozayemon remained unexhausted.

" Like all noted amateurs, Gozayemon would probably have found imitators in later times. Yet had it not been for an accident, his name would certainly be little remembered outside the circle of connoisseurs of whose somewhat archaic creed he was so obedient a disciple, and in whose hands his comparatively scanty productions remained. That accident was the discovery—about the year 1830—of a recipe which he had employed in the manufacture of his enamels. The document containing the precious formula had found its way into the possession of a dealer in *bric-a-brac* who lived at Kuwana, and whose son, Mori Yusetsu, had already gained some distinction as an imitator of *Raku* faience. Fully appreciating the value of the knowledge thus strangely acquired, Yusetsu immediately set himself to profit by it, and in order to give his counterfeit ware a greater semblance of authenticity, he persuaded Gozayemon's grandson to sell him the *Banko* stamp. Thus the works of the Ise amateur were again brought into public notice, and that rather by a freak of fortune than by any public knowledge of their merits. Yusetsu, however, was saved from performing the ignoble role of a mere imitator by his quickness of observation, for, detecting that the Chinese artists—whose works, like Gozayemon, he took as his models—used moulds applied internally for their more elaborate pieces, he immediately adopted that method in his own workshop, and so caused the name of *Banko*—for he still continued to employ Gozayemon's stamp—to be associated with the introduction of a valuable novelty in Japanese Keramics. It has already been noticed that the Kyôtô artist, Mokubei, was the first to follow the Chinese example in the matter of moulds, but, whereas he fashioned his clay *in* the mould, Yusetsu reversed the process by putting the mould inside the vase and pressing the clay with the hand into the matrix. The consequence is that his pieces carry their designs on the inner as well as the outer surface, and are, moreover, thumb-marked. Of course a mould thus employed was necessarily constructed on principles different from those which governed the Kyôtô process. Accordingly, we find that the mould of Yusetsu, instead of being simply divided into two parts, was built up of six, eight, or sometimes twelve, longitudinal sections, which were withdrawn one by one after they had accomplished their end. The results displayed such clever modelling that they subsequently came to be regarded as representative pieces of *Banko-yaki*. In fact, it is through the works of Yusetsu, or rather through the methods he devised, that the Ise ware has attained the wide-spread popularity it now enjoys; nor that undeservedly either, for some of the designs of his school exhibit a remarkable combination of artistic and technical excellence. Particularly worthy of mention are pieces ornamented with storks, dragons, and so forth, in relief, and others with clever arabesques in coloured slips on a green or rich brown ground. All the *Yusetsu Banko* ware is faience, and the specimens are sometimes stamped '*Yusetsu.*' Among his productions, a variety which often passes, or is made to pass, for '*Ko-Banko*' is a finely-crackled faience of a dark cream tint, decorated with blue under the glaze, and above it with a preponderance of red diapers, among which are reserved medallions containing landscapes or mythical subjects. Pieces in this style bear a considerable resemblance to the modern *Akahada-yaki*, but even in the absence of marks the two may be readily distinguished, not only by the omission of the blue in the latter, but also by its denser *pâte* and the yellowish tinge of the body-glaze. The collector will generally be safe in attributing specimens of this nature to Yusetsu. Yuyeki, originally called Yohei, a younger brother of Yusetsu, was also an able artist—better, indeed, than Yusetsu himself, according to some authorities—and Mori Yogozayemon, the present representative of the family, still carries on the manufacture. The reader will perceive, however, that in the hands of Yusetsu and his successors the *Banko* ware underwent a complete change of character."—From BRINKLEY's *History of Japanese Keramics*.

No. 361.—Cup. Diameter, 3½ in. Depth, 3 in.

> Body glaze, a reddish white, crackled. Decorated with archaic designs, flowers and a bird, in red and green. Imitation of the old Chinese painted porcelain. Date, 1770. Mark, *Banko*.

No. 362.—Bowl, with narrow base. Diameter, 6½ in. Depth, 4 in.

> The outside is covered with a light green glaze, finely crackled, and has floral scrolls in high relief. The inside is covered with a buff glaze, crackled and much stained from use. Growing over the rim into the interior are boughs of camellia, and chrysanthemum in green, red, blue, and yellow. Date, 1780. Mark, *Banko*.

No. 363.—Bowl, with high base, the upper portion being in the form of a coiled Dragon. Diameter, 7 in. Height, 4¼ in.

> The inside is covered with light green glaze: the outside with a mottled glaze, pink, black, and white. Date, 1790. Mark, *Banko*.

No. 364.—Incense Box, square. Height, 1½ in. Side, 1¼ in.

> Covered with a cream-coloured finely crackled glaze. The decoration is in dark red under the glaze, and consists of branches of plum, bamboo, and chrysanthemum on the side, and an archaic design on the top. Date, 1770. Mark, *Banko*.

No. 365.—Incense Holder, in the form of an ox lying down. Length, 3 in. Breadth, 1¾ in. Height, 2 in.

> The body of the ox is covered with a golden brown glaze; the lower half of the box with a rich green. Date, 1770. Mark, *Banko*.

No. 366.—Bottle, with tapering body and narrow neck. Height, 7½ in. Diameter, 3½ in.

> Covered with a dark blue glaze running into green at the shoulder and base. Date, 1790. Mark, *Banko*.

No. 367.—Wine Holder, with handle and spout. Height, 6½ in. Diameter, 6½ in.

> Covered with a grass green glaze running into rich blue round the neck. Made by Yusetsu Banko. Mark, *Banko*.

No. 368.—Wine Vessel, with spout and handle. Height, 7 in. Diameter, 5 in.

> Covered with a cream coloured glaze, finely crackled. On the sides are large medallions containing landscapes in green, brown and blue enamels. These medallions are divided by a broad band of red, in which are reserved small medallions with conventional designs and various forms of the characters *ju* (congratulation) and *fuku* (prosperity). On the spout and handle are leaf scrolls in red, green, and blue enamels. Round the neck is a band of blue diaper under the glaze, and above this a band of scallop in green, red, and blue enamels. Made by Yusetsu Banko. Mark, *Banko*.

No. 369.—Wine Vessel, with spout and handle. Height, 10½ in. Diameter, 3½ in.

> Decoration similar to that of No. 368. Maker and mark, also the same.

No. 370.—Candlestick, with spreading base and narrow neck. Height, 9 in.

> Covered with a grayish white glaze, coarsely crackled and running into blue where it lies thickest. Decoration entirely in red. Round the base, circular medallions with conventional *Shishi*, *Howo*, and flowers. Between the medallions are leaf scrolls. On the neck are bands of scallops and lines. Same maker, and mark as No. 368.

No. 371.—Incense Box, in the form of Clam Shell. Length, 3½ in. Breadth, 3 in.

> Covered with a reddish brown glaze, on which are chrysanthemums and *Kiri* in white slip, forming Imperial crest. Mark, *Yusetsu*. Made by Yusetsu Banko.

No. 372.—Dish, circular. Diameter, 7 in. Depth, 2 in.

> Body glaze, a reddish white. The outside is plain; the inside covered with decoration, viz., in the middle a large medallion, with three children at play, and various diapers: round this medallion are three bands of diapers, and above these a broad band of red with silver scrolls. The colours are red and gold. Mark, in a square, *Akogi no hen* (*i. e.*, name of place of manufacture) and beside this the characters *Ran yen gwa* (painted by *Ran yen*). Date, 1860. This piece was specially made for presentation to the Daimiyo Seishû (Ise).

AWAJI WARE.

"A ware of which considerable quantities have found their way westward, of late years, is the *Awaji-yaki* so called from an island of the same name, where it is manufactured at the village of Iga. It was first produced between the years 1830 and 1840 by one Kajû Mimpei, who had acquired his technical knowledge in Kyôtô. His pieces—pottery at first but afterwards stone-ware or porcelain—were covered sometimes with single-coloured, sometimes with variegated glazes. Among the latter, a favourite, is that known as the "tortoise-shell" glaze (*Bekko-de*), the colours employed, being yellow, green, white, and brownish purple, which are disposed in tolerably regular patches. The effect is brilliant, but by no means æsthetic. Neither is the idea original. A similar arrangement of coloured glazes—purple and turquoise-blue—is to be found in the faience of the potters of Chôsa during the 17th century, and in the porcelain of the celebrated Zengoro Hozen, who in his turn copied from Chinese artists. Of single-coloured glazes the chief varieties met with in the *Awaji-yaki* are green and yellow, the finest pieces of all being those in which the body is yellow and the design green, after the fashion of the well-known "Imperial yellow" of China. It need scarcely be observed that the exquisitely delicate canary-yellow of the Chinese porcelain is not to be found in any Japanese ware; the best imitations achieved by Mimpei are straw-coloured. He did not confine himself to the production of monochrome or variegated glazes. Many of his pieces were decorated in the style of the Kyôtô school. The *pâte* of the *Awaji-yaki* varies considerably. Sometimes we find pottery of a chocolate-brown colour, hard, but not very close; sometimes stone-ware, light gray, very fine, and smooth to the touch; sometimes porcelain. Mimpei was succeeded by his son Rikitaro and his nephew Sampei, who still carry on the manufacture, though their works will not compare with those of Mimpei himself."—From BRINKLEY'S *History of Japanese Keramics*.

No. 373.—Figure of Oto Gozen. Porcelain. Height, 2½ in.

    Face and hands unglazed. Hair black. Drapery yellow with floral scrolls in gold and medallions of diaper in green and red. Mark *Mimpei*. Made by Kajû Mimpei. (From the collection of Ninagawa Noritane.)

No. 374.—Cup. Faience. Diameter, 4 in. Depth, 3 in.

    Body glaze, cream white, crackled. Decoration a bunch of flowers and leaves delicately executed in green, black, gold, red, pink, and purple. Mark, *Mimpei*. Same maker as No. 373.

No. 375.—Incense Burner. Height, 7 in. Diameter, 8 in.
> Porcelain. Covered with a canary-yellow glaze; crackled, and having two dragons and clouds incised. Delicately cut Silver Lid. Same maker as No. 374.

No. 376.—Bowl. Diameter, 6 in. Depth, 2¼ in.
> Porcelain. Covered with a rich mustard-yellow glaze, and decorated with flowers and leaves in green, white and purple. Same maker as No. 374.

No. 377.—Bowl. Diameter, 5¾ in. Depth, 3 in.
> Porcelain. Covered with green, purple, yellow, and white glazes, run in patches to imitate tortoise-shell. Mark, an illegible character in blue. Same maker as No. 374.

IZUMO WARE.

"Few wares are more widely and deservedly appreciated in the European markets than that produced of late years at Fujina, in the province of Izumo. It is a pottery covered with a pale yellow or straw-coloured glaze, which forms a background of peculiar delicacy for the enamel and gold decoration. The designs, however, are not by any means executed in exceptional style, partly, no doubt, from lack of good painters - a want that has generally been noticeable in the productions of Izumo—but partly also because the surface of the soft sensitive faience is ill-adapted to the reception of vitrifiable materials, and especially to that of gold, which is at once the most essential and the most refractory of the decorative agents. The polishing of the metallic oxides, which on their emergence from the kiln present an appearance the very reverse of ornamental, has always been an operation of considerable difficulty in Japanese Keramic manufacture. Zengoro Hozen (Eiraku), who was notably successful in this respect, is said to have invariably entrusted the process to little children, finding that from their hands alone gentleness of touch could be certainly obtained. Somewhat difficult to reconcile with this idea is the fact that a wisp of straw was preferred as a burnisher; but it would appear that straw possesses certain properties peculiarly suitable for such a purpose, seeing that in Satsuma and elsewhere a bag filled with that material chopped fine and mixed with rice-husks has long been similarly employed. Improved processes may perhaps one day correct a certain lack of intimacy that now seems to exist between the glaze and the decoration of the *Izumo-yaki*, in which event the faience would certainly occupy a very high place among Japanese productions."—From BRINKLEY's *History of Japanese Keramics*.

No. 378.—Tea Jar. Height, 3¼ in. Diameter, 2¼ in.

    Pottery. The upper portion covered with an iron red, speckled glaze. Date, 1760. Made by order of the celebrated *Chajin* Sôchiu. *Rakuzan* ware.

No. 379.—Tea Jar. Height, 2½ in. Diameter, 3¼ in.

    The upper portion covered with a reddish brown glaze speckled with gold. Date, 1800. (From the collection of Ninagawa Noritane.) *Rakuzan* ware.

No. 380.—Tea Jar. Height, 4 in. Diameter, 2½ in.

    Covered with an iron red glaze flecked with dark blue. Date, 1800. *Rakuzan* ware.

No. 381.—Cup. Diameter, 4 in. Depth, 3 in.

    Body glaze, a brownish white, with roughly executed floral decoration in green, red, blue, and white. Date, 1770. (From the collection of Ninagawa Noritane.) This specimen illustrates the Izumo potters' earliest essays in enamel decoration.

No. 382.—Flower Vase, with tapering body and narrow neck. Height, 5 in. Diameter, 2½ in.

    Stone-ware. Body glaze, a brownish white. Decoration, trees, flowers, and a bird delicately executed in green, red, purple, and gold enamels. Made by order of Funai, Duke of Dewa, and painted by Zenshiro. Date, 1820.

No. 383.—Tea Holder. Height, 2½ in. Diameter, 2¼ in.

    Body glaze, yellow. Decoration, delicately executed floral design in green, blue, red, and gold. Date, 1830.

No. 384.—Cup. Diameter, 4½ in. Depth, 3¼ in.

    Body glaze, milk white. Round the sides are four circular medallions of delicately executed floral subjects in red, green, pink, white, and gold. Round the rim, outside, is a band of diapers, and inside a band of *Howo* and clouds. Date, 1830.

No. 385.—Cup. Diameter, 5¼ in. Depth, 3¼ in.

    Body glaze, a brownish white, finely crackled. Decoration, floral subject in green, red, and gold. Date, 1820.

No. 386.—Incense Box. Diameter, 1¾ in. Depth, 1 in.

    Body glaze, yellow. Decoration, Imperial crest in gold. Date, 1820.

No. 387.—Cup. Diameter, 4½ in. Depth, 3½ in.

    Body glaze, milk white. Round the rim a band of diapers in green, red, yellow, and blue enamels. On the sides are delicately executed chrysanthemums in the same colours. Date, 1840.

TAKATORI WARE (STONE WARE).

"The Keramic industry of Japan was largely influenced by the advent of the Korean potters who came over in the train of the *Taiko's* generals. Of these imported experts the most successful, from a technical point of view, were those who settled at Takatori, in Chikuzen, a province lying on the north of Hizen, and forming, in the early days of the seventeenth century, the fief of a nobleman, Kuroda Nagamasa, whose relations with the Court at Kyôtô, and subsequently with that at Yedo, were particularly close. Of the exact number of Koreans who were located at Takatori we have no record, but the names of two, Shinkuro and Hachizo, have been preserved as masters of the art. The latter is said to have been among the prisoners taken by the Lord of Chikuzen, and the former to have been specially selected by Kato Kiyomasa, general-in-chief of the expedition, as a potter already renowned in Korea. The names Shinkuro and Hachizo were, of course, given to them in Japan. What they were originally called tradition does not say, but it is on record that both were natives of a Korean village known by the Japanese as Ido. There is no question that the potter's industry had been practised in Chikuzen long before the coming of these men. Ancient annals mention ware produced there as early as the ninth century, but it was probably unglazed pottery, without any claim to public favour. That the resources of the place were meagre has been inferred from the fact that Shinkuro and Hachizo, during the early years of their residence at Takatori, used imported materials only. It seems to have been a part of the *Taiko's* order to his generals, that not workmen alone but also matter to work with should be brought from Korea. Chikuzen certainly did not want for fine clays, as was proved by the pieces subsequently manufactured there. The first production of Shinkuro and Hâchizo at Takatori were in the pure Korean style, the shapes and ornamentation being rococo in character; the *pâte* coarse; the glaze thin and diaphanous. Shinkuro did not long remain a captive. He died almost immediately after the lord of the province, Kuroda Nagamasa. The latter's son, Tadayuki, showed himself a liberal patron of art. It happened at the time of which we write that the celebrated dilettante Kobori Masakazu, feudal chief of Yenshu, interested himself in the work of the Korean captives, and to him, at Fushimi, near Kyôtô, Tadayuki sent Hachizo and the latter's son, Hachiroyemon, for instruction. Even this temporary association with the great amateur would probably have been sufficient to establish the prestige of the Takatori ware. But, in addition, Hachizo was shortly afterwards assisted by a workman of incomparably greater skill and finer artistic instincts than himself. This was Igarashi Jizayemon, a native of Hizen, who had devoted several years to acquiring and practising the processes of the Seto potters of Owari. He appears to have been a sort of "gentleman at large," wandering from place to place in his capacity of amateur artist. Happening to visit Chikuzen, he was speedily taken under Tadayuki's protection, and appointed conjointly with Hachizo, to superintend the factory at Takatori. Previously to this event the *Takatori-yaki* potters, under the direction of Hachizo and Shinkuro, had applied only one coat of glaze to their pieces. They made no attempt to copy the multiple glazes of the Seto artists. But with Igarashi's advent a new era commenced. The *Takatori-yaki* very soon rose to conspicuous eminence among Japanese ware for the lustre, variety and general beauty of its glazes.

"Their weight in gold proved often but a fraction of their worth in the eyes of subsequent generations, for they became the representatives, not merely of names great in the history of Keramics, but also of a creed reverenced by every student of art in succeeding centuries. In truth a man must needs bear all this in mind at his first introduction to the treasures of a Japanese collection, else will he run much risk of losing his gravity when he sees deferential fingers carefully extract from brocade-wrappers and cases of fine lacquer a tiny pot, sober-hued, and, it may be, roughly finished, which to the uninitiated seems scarcely worthy to serve as an apothecary's phial, but has, nevertheless, for its possessor beauties as inexplicable as the charms of the Japanese dance with its strange music of motion, palpable only to Eastern senses.

"The history of the Takatori potters shows that they frequently changed the site of their factory, doubtless in search of good clay. Thus in 1614, we find them at Iso; in 1630, at Shirahata-yama; in 1662, at Tsutsumi-mura; a little later, at Tajima-mura and Shimo-keigo-mura. Finally, in 1708, they moved to Shikahara-mura (stag-plain village)—always, of course, keeping within the province of Chikuzen—and there, establishing a factory on the slope of Uyeno-yama, manufactured censers, tea-cups, water-vessels, incense-boxes, &c., so skilfully and in such quantities that the place ultimately received the name of Higashi-sara-yama, or Eastern Plate-Hill. A few years later (1716), another factory was established in the neighborhood, under the name of Nishi-sara-yama (Western Plate-Hill). The productions of the latter were coarser and destined for commoner use than those of the former. These various changes of locality may be traced, with more or less accuracy, in the *pâte* of the ware. Thus, the collector may accept it as a rule that the clay of the Early period (1600–1660) *Takatori-yaki* is of a light gray colour (called by the Japanese *nezumi-iro*, or mouse-color); that of the Middle period (1660-1700), nearly white; that of the Third period (1700–1800), reddish, and sometimes purplish. It will not, however, be safe to conclude that every specimen having a nearly white *pâte* dates from a period prior to 1700. All that can be confidently asserted is that such a *pâte* does not belong to an era earlier than 1660. Considering the qualities of the *Takatori-yaki*, the notice it has hitherto received at the hands of Western commentators is singularly meagre. Among specimens produced during the third period of manufacture are to be found cleverly modelled figures of mythological beings and animals, covered with lustrous variegated glazes, the general colours being gray or buff, with tints of green, chocolate, brown and sometimes blue. These have always been favourites with buyers of bric-a-bric, and many of them are doubtless to be found in Western collections. It may be mentioned that a popular distinction is made in Japan between the earliest specimens of Takatori ware and those manufactured subsequent to the instruction received from Kobori Masakazu (born 1576, died 1645): the former are called *Ko-Takatori* (old Takatori); the latter *Yenshû-Takatori*."—From BRINKLEY's *History of Japanese Keramics*.

No. 388.—Figure of Chinese Sage. Height, 13 in.

    Face, unglazed; tunic, covered with a rich iron red glaze, flecked with black, trousers with a green glaze. Date, 1640.

No. 389.—Incense Burner, in the form of an Owl sitting on a Roof of Grass. Height, 9½.

    The owl is covered with an iron red glaze; the roof with green. Mark, *Taka* in a circle, and the characters *Shigechika* (name of Maker). Date 1830.

No. 390.—Tea Jar. Height, 2½ in. Diameter, 2 in.

    Covered with a light brown glaze, having white and blue flecks. Date, 1750.

No. 391.—Bottle-shaped Vase. Height, 13 in. Diameter, 6 in.

    Covered with a rich glaze of various tints, blue, green, and golden brown. Date, 1780.

No. 392.—Figure of God Fukurokujin, forming Incense-burner. Height, 12¼ in.

    Covered with a rich glaze of brown, blue, and green tints. Mark, *Taka* in a circle, and the characters *Hide-moto* (name of maker). Date, 1790.

No. 393.—Water Holder. Length, 3½ in. Breadth, 2½ in.

    Covered with a rich glaze of green, blue, and brown tints. Date, 1760.

No. 394.—Dish, in the form of a Lotus Leaf with rolled edges.

> Covered outside with a rich brown glaze, having metallic spots; inside, with a green glaze. Mark, *Ki* (initial character of maker's name).

No. 395.—Figure of the Genius Tekkai, seated on a Rock and blowing out his spirit. Height, 8½ in.

> Covered with a rich glaze of green, blue, white, and brown tints. Mark, *Taka* in a circle, and the characters *Hokiu* (name of maker). Date, 1800.

No. 396.—Vase, with swelling shoulders and tapering waist. Height, 15 in. Diameter of shoulder, 8 in.

> Covered above with a white glaze which runs into green and then into black. Date, 1820.

No. 397.—Incense Burner, with gilt top and three feet. Height, 3 in. Diameter, 3 in.

> Covered with an iron-red glaze, finely speckled, and having a streak of green and black. By the celebrated Takatori potter Hachizo.

KISHÛ WARE.

ONIWA-YAKI, OR KAIRAKU-YEN-YAKI.

"A little more than half a mile westward of Wakayama, in the province of Kishû, stood formerly the country residence of the family whose representatives governed the district. Within the park of this Nishihama, at the beginning of the present century, Tokugawa Harunori, then head of the family, caused a private kiln to be built for the manufacture of porcelain decorated with blue under the glaze. We have seen that the porcelain industry, as distinguished from that of pottery and faience, received a notable impulse in the opening years of the nineteenth century. The Nishihama factory is an example of this development. Very little is known of its first productions. They were completely lost sight of when, in 1827, Harunori, after one of his periodical visits to Kyôto, brought back with him the already-renowned Keramist, Zengoro Hozen. The character of the Kishû-yaki immediately underwent a complete change. Zengoro had made his name by imitating the brilliant glazes of Cochin-China, and to this species of work he applied himself at Harunori's factory. The outcome of the kiln was thenceforth known as *O-niwa-yaki* (ware of the honourable park) or *Kairaku-yen-yaki* (ware of the park of ease and fellowship). The *pâte*, sometimes white, sometimes a reddish gray, was very fine, varying from porcelain to faience, but being for the most part a hard stone-ware. The glazes were remarkably rich and beautiful: purple, green, turquoise, yellow, and white. They were employed in various ways. Perhaps the most common was a purple ground covered with scroll-work in relief, portions of the scroll being filled with turquoise blue. In other and more excellent pieces we find a rich green ground marbled with purple, or decorated with medallions in yellow, purple, white, and blue. Glazes showing greater richness, lustre, and purity of colour were never produced by any Japanese potter. Harunori loaded Zengoro with favours, and bestowed on him three seals; two of silver, bearing the inscriptions *Kairaku-yen* and *Eiraku*, and one of gold, inscribed *Kahin Shiriu*. Japanese antiquaries say that the term *Kahin Shiriu* (branch of *Kahin*) has reference to the earliest pottery of China, which, according to them, was manufactured by an artist called Chun at the kiln of Kahin (Chinese *Hopin*), about 4,000 years ago. This point is involved in obscurity. Eiraku, as we have already explained, is the Japanese pronunciation of the Chinese period *Yung-lo* (1403-1425), during which was first produced the celebrated "rouge vif" with decorations in gold. Zengoro never allowed any specimen to leave his hands bearing the stamp *Kahin Shiriu* unless he was thoroughly satisfied with the success of his work. Sometimes he added the mark *Eiraku*, and in many cases his imitations of the Chinese turquoise-blues and purples are stamped simply "*Kairaku-yen*." He generally worked to order, and it is said to have been his habit to manufacture from five to ten specimens of any piece which he had undertaken to produce. Of these the best was chosen, and the remainder were destroyed in the presence of the person who had ordered them. He appears to have remained some eight or nine years in Kishû, and after his return to Kyôtô the Nishihama factory was placed under the direction of another workman from the Western capital, by name Yoshihei. It would appear, however, that Zengoro's glazes were not to be compassed by any other expert. The Kairaku ware gradually lost its high character, and on Harunori's death, in 1844, the manufacture came to an end."—From BRINKLEY's *History of Japanese Keramics*.

No. 398.—Vase, with spreading neck and lion-shaped handles. Height, 14½ in.

> *Meppo* ware. Covered with a celadon (green) glaze. The lower part has dragons, clouds, and diapers, partly in relief, partly incised. The body is covered with leaves and flowers in high relief. The neck has archaic designs incised. Mark, *Zuishi* (name of kiln). Date, 1810.

No. 399.—Figure of Genius and Rat. Height, 6½ in.

> Covered with celadon (green) glaze. Mark, *Nanki Otoko-yama* in blue (*Nanki* is another name for Kishû, and *Otoko-yama* is the name of the kiln); and the characters *Sem-ba* in a circle (maker's name). Date, 1820.

No. 400.—Vase, pierced for hanging. Height, 6½ in. Diameter, 3¼ in.

> Body glaze, a rich purple, with archaic designs in turquoise blue in relief. Mark, *Kai-raku yen-sei*. Made at *Kai-raku-yen*). Date, 1820.

No. 401.—Bowl. Diameter, 6¾ in. Depth, 2½ in.

> Covered with rich purple and turquoise-blue glazes in patches. Date, 1830.

No. 402.—Bowl. Diameter, 5 in. Depth, 2 in.

> Covered with turquoise-blue glaze. Mark, *Kairaku-yen-sei* (Made at Kairakuyen). Date, 1830.

No. 402A.—Vase. Height, 22½ in. Diameter, 11 in.

> Porcelain, covered with celadon-green glaze. The upper and lower portions are fluted horizontically and vertically. Round the middle is a band of peonies and leaves in relief. Date, 1830.

SANDA WARE (CELADON). (STONE WARE.)

"The province of Setsu lies at the head of the Izumi-nada, which may be called the northern entrance to the Inland Sea. It contains the flourishing city of Osaka and the foreign settlement of Kôbe. For many years Osaka has occupied the first place among the Keramic marts of Japan, and to this day its *bric-a-brac* shops have no equals elsewhere in the empire. Yet the province possesses few Keramic factories worthy of note. The principal is that of *Sanda*, established about the year 1690, by order of Kuki, lord of the district. The early *Sanda-yaki* was a pottery closely resembling that of Tamba (*vide Tamba-yaki*), but towards the end of the eighteenth century two workmen, Uchigami and Ippei, succeeded in making themselves acquainted with the porcelain methods of Arita. Their ambition apparently was to copy Chinese celadon, but it was not till they obtained from Kyôtô the assistance of Shûhei, Kumachichi, and Kamesuke, pupils of the celebrated Rokubei, that they accomplished anything worthy of note. Then, indeed, their imitations of the much-esteemed "sea-green" became so excellent that the achievements of all other artists in this regard were forgotten, and the term *Sanda-seiji* gradually passed into a synonym for Japanese celadon. It may be well, however, to remind the reader that more than a century before the appearance of the *Sanda-seiji* a celadon of much better quality had been produced at the Hizen factories under the special patronage of Nabeshima, lord of the province. It would therefore appear that the celebrity enjoyed by the celadon of Setsu was in some degree a question of quantity, for while the outcome of the Hizen workshops in this particular variety was very small, being in fact confined to pieces for special use or presentation purposes, that of Sanda was abundant. In colour the *Sanda-seiji* is a bright green, lacking the warmth of the Chinese *Schichi-kan-seiji* and the delicacy of the Nabeshima ware."—From BRINKLEY's *History of Japanese Keramics*.

No. 403.—Figure of Hotei, with bag and children. Height, 10 in.

    The face, arms, and breast are unglazed. The rest of the piece covered with a sea-green glaze. Date, 1700.

No. 404.—Vase, with circular body and flat faces. Height, 9 in. Diameter, 8 in.

    Covered with a light-green glaze. On the faces are a dragon and *Howo*, with various diapers; on the sides leaves and flowers: the whole of the decoration is in relief. Date, 1780.

No. 405.—Vase, with spreading neck and base. Height, 8½ in.

    Covered with a rich green glaze. Date, 1830.

No. 406.—Bonbon Box, with Cover. Height, 2½ in. Diameter, 2½ in.

    Covered with a light green glaze. Date, 1820.

No. 406A.—Figure of Kirin. Height, 31 in.

    Finely modelled, and covered with a rich green glaze. Date, 1780.

TAMBA WARE (POTTERY).

"In the province of Tamba, which lies to the west of Yamashiro, pottery is said to have been manufactured as early as the sixth century of our era. It was a coarse, unglazed, and meritless production. Not until the time when the *Taiko's* influence imparted so much activity to the art-industries of Japan did the ware assume any features worthy of note. Pieces after the fashion of the rude faience of Korea then made their appearance. The workshop—which was at a place called Onohara—was brought into some notice by a peculiar faience with blisters on its surface, which was supposed to resemble an imported ware attributed to Siam. In general, however, the Tamba potters of those days took the *Seto-yaki* as their model. Among their tea-jars, cups, and water-vessels, specimens with a very hard, reddish brown *pâte*, and chocolate, black, or mahogany coloured glazes are most frequently met with. About the middle of the seventeenth century the factory was moved to a place called Tachikui, and from that time its productions were known as *Tachikui-yaki*. They have but little interest for Western collectors, though occasionally one finds splashed glazes not without attractions. The first workman of Tamba who distinguished himself by the production of good faience is said to have been a man named Kichizo.

"Early in the present century, under the auspices of Kutzuki, feudal chief of the district, a factory established at Sasayama, also in the province of Tamba, began to turn out pieces of greatly improved description. The paste was carefully manipulated, and the decoration—sometimes applied in the form of *pâte sur pâte* to an unglazed surface, and sometimes enamelled in the ordinary method—was generally of a very artistic nature, the subjects being copied directly from the works of the celebrated painter Okyo. The best specimens of this period are those stamped with the name of Nosaka, the only one of the Tamba workmen who seems to have marked his productions."—From BRINKLEY'S *History of Japanese Keramics*.

No. 407.—Tea Jar. Height, 3 in. Diameter, 2¾ in.
    Covered with a mottled glaze of brown and black. On the box are the characters *Oyeyama* in gold. Date, 1620.

No. 408.—Wine Bottles, two. Height, 7¼ in. Diameter, 3½ in.
    Made of a fine, gray clay, unglazed. Decoration, two storks, in white and black. This ware is known as *Sasayama-yaki* or *Tachikui-yaki*. Date, 1820. (From the collection of Ninagawa Noritane.)

No. 409.—Vase. Height, 5 in. Diameter, 2½ in.
Body glaze, black with faint silver lines in imitation of the Chinese *Temmoku* ware. Decoration, a floral design in gold. Mark, *Chigai-yama Nao saku.* (Made by Nao Chigai-yama.) Same ware and date as No. 408. (From the collection of Ninagawa Noritane.)

SETO WARE.

TOSHIRO-YAKI OR SETO-YAKI.

"The province of Owari, or Bishiu, is full of interest for the student, whether for the sake of its association with the great name of Kato Shirozayemon (commonly called Tôshiro), or because its manufactures were sufficiently pre eminent to become a synonym—*Seto-mono*—for all Keramic productions in Japan. It has already been related how Shirozayemon visited China in 1223, and what improved processes he there acquired. The pieces he had previously produced did not possess one redeeming feature, nor need they be cited except as illustrations of the very small progress Japan had made in Keramics up to that time. They were thick, clumsily shaped, and unglazed at the orifice, so that even the Japanese *Cha-jin* who treasures them to-day with such enthusiasm, is at a loss to point out any merit justifying his affection. Amongst these specimens of "*Ko-seto*" (old Seto), as they are called, a curious example of the fictitious value which subsequent generations attach to the great master's handiwork, is afforded by the variety "*Hori-dashi-te*" or "dug-out ware." It consists of pieces which, having been rejected from time to time on account of technical defects until their inconvenient accumulation suggested the expedient of burying them in the ground, were dug out two or three centuries later and placed among the treasures of the Tea-clubs, the faults that rendered them worthless seven hundred years ago being condoned to-day for the sake of their associations. Previously to his visit to China, Tôshiro's wares were stoved in an inverted position, so that the orifices were unglazed. For this reason they are subsequently called *Kuchi-hagi-de*, or bared (*hagi*) orifice (*kuchi*) variety (*te*). Another distinguishing appellation was *Atsu-de*, or thick variety—a term which explains itself. It is unnecessary to describe them at length. They were nothing more than coarse pottery, made of iron-red clay, covered with clumsily applied glaze, sometimes black, sometimes brown, sometimes a reddish gray, and occasionally having a tinge of yellow.

After Tôshiro's return from China his pottery showed a marked improvement both in form and finish. He now produced dainty little tea jars, of close, fine *pâte*, excellently manipulated. The thick, clumsy character of his former efforts disappeared entirely. His pieces were no longer stoved in an inverted position, so that their edges, instead of being bare and fringed with irregular patches of glaze, were smooth and fairly finished. His glazes were lustrous and free from discontinuities and irregularities. Their colours were black, amber-brown, chocolate, and yellowish gray. Very soon this *Tôshiro-yaki* became the rage. The feudal barons, who had adopted the fashion set by Yoritomo of rewarding the services of their vassals with presents of powdered tea, then a rare luxury, chose Tôshiro's jars to contain these gifts, so that the reputation of the Seto potter was quickly established. Connoisseurs decided, and the decision has never been revoked, that his best pieces were those with a purplish *pâte*; his second-best those with a light-red *pâte*; his third-best those with a gray *pâte*, and that the *pâte* of the least value was dark-red. Another point of merit, scarcely appreciable to foreign eyes, was the *ito-giri*, or trace of the thread used to cut off the superfluous clay at the bottom of the piece, before removing the latter from the wheel. The spiral thus formed is supposed to afford some subtle indication of the potter's skill.

Tôshiro's factory was known as "*Heishi-gama*," so called because its staple production had previously been the "*Heishi*" (a sort of wine-jar). After the materials he had brought from China were exhausted, he began to use Japanese clay, and the pieces he then manufactured are called by some connoisseurs "*Ko-seto*," which term would thus include the ware which preceded, as well as that which succeeded, his visit to China. But the truth is that much confusion exists among the Japanese themselves on this question of nomenclature, some experts preferring to give the name "*Karamomo*" or "*Kambutsu*" (Chinese ware) to the pieces Toshiro made with Chinese materials after his return to Japan, while others call this variety "*Tobutsu*."

Toshiro, in after life, changed his name to Shunkei, and the pieces he then manufactured are called "*Shunkei-yaki*." They are accounted his *chefs d'œuvre*.

It would be difficult to convey to the reader an adequate impression of the esteem in which choice specimens of *Tôshiro-yaki* are held in Japan. They are swathed in coverings of the costliest brocade and kept in boxes of superb lacquer. There is scarcely any limit to the prices paid for them, and the names of their fortunate owners are spoken of with respect by *Chajin* of a proper spirit."—From BRINKLEY's *History of Japanese Keramics*.

No. 410.—Tea Jar. Height, 2½ in. Diameter, 2 in.

> Covered with a black glaze slightly mottled. Made by Kato Shirozayemom, commonly known as Toshiro. Date, 1225. (From the collection of Ninagawa Noritane.)

No. 411.—Tea Jar. Height, 3 in. Diameter, 2½ in.

> The upper half covered with a buff-coloured glaze, crackled. Made by Toshiro, son of Kato Shirozayemon. Date, 1245. This ware is a specimen of the class known as *Manako Tobutsu*, to distinguish it from the manufacturers of Shirozayemon, which are called *Tobutsu*. (From the collection of Ninagawa Noritane.)

No. 412.—Tea Jar. Height, 3¼ in. Diameter, 2¼ in.

> Beautifully finished, and covered with a reddish brown glaze passing into black on the shoulder. Made by the third Toshiro. Date, 1350. A specimen of the ware known as *Chiu-kobutsu* or *Kinkazan*.

No. 413.—Tea Jar. Height, 2¼ in. Diameter, 3½ in.

> The upper half is covered with a golden brown glaze running into light buff and metallic black. Made by the fourth Toshiro. Date, 1380. A specimen of the ware called *Hafugama*.

No. 414.—Tea Jar. Height, 4 in. Diameter, 2 in.

> Covered with a pinkish white glaze, crackled, and having a leaf spray in metallic black together with the characters *Utsu seme karagoromo* (name given to this tea-jar at the time of its manufacture). Made by the celebrated *Chajin*, Shino Iyenobu. Date, 1480.

No. 415.—Tea Jar. Height, 2½ in. Diameter, 3 in.

> Covered with a reddish brown glaze flecked with large metallic spots. Made by Koson. Date, 1475.

No. 416.—Tea Jar. Height, 2½ in. Diameter, 3 in.

> Covered with light iron-red glaze, flecked with large metallic spots. Date, 1570. Made to order of the celebrated *Chajin*, Oribe.

No. 417.—Bon-bon Holder, square in section, with tapering neck and base. Height, 3 in. Side, 2½ in.

> Covered with a rich green glaze. On the sides are designs in relief representing the Seven Sages in a bamboo grove, and diapers. Made to order of Oribe. Date, 1580.

No. 418.—Flower Vase, with globular body, narrow neck, and spreading Lid. Height, 7 in. Diameter, 3½ in.

> Body glaze, iron red flecked with metallic spots. Date, 1650. A specimen of the ware known as *Nochi Shunkei*.

No. 419.—Vase, with globular body and tapering neck. Height, 9½ in. Diameter, 4½ in.

> Covered with a dark brown glaze flecked on the neck with tea-green. Date, 1700.

No. 420.—Vase, with swelling waist and trumpet-shaped base and neck. Height, 12½ in. Diameter of body, 3½ in.

> The body is decorated with a scroll of peonies in high relief. The handles are lion's heads with loose rings. The whole is covered with a yellow glaze, crackled. Date, 1700. *Ki-seto* ware.

No. 421.—*Figure of the Genius Gama, seated, with a Frog on his shoulder. Height, 16½ in. *Minato* faience.

> The face, breast, hands, and legs are unglazed; the rest of the piece covered with a light green glaze. Mark, illegible. Date, 1800.

No. 422.—Tea Jar. Height, 3 in. Diameter, 2¼ in.

> White porcelain, with floral designs in blue under the glaze. Made by Tomikichi, the first manufacturer of porcelain in Owari.

No. 423.—Incense Box. Diameter, 2½ in. Depth, 1 in.

> Porcelain. Decorated with archaic designs in white on a rich blue ground. Made by Hansuke, a fellow workman of Tomikichi and the best maker of blue and white china Owari has produced.

No. 424.—Square Seal, with fabulous animal (*Kirin*) for handle. Height, 3¼ in. Side of square, 3 in.

> White porcelain finely modelled. By Sosendo, a fellow workman of Hansuke, renowned for his skill in modelling.

No. 425.—Square Seal, the handle in the form of a tortoise, with an old man (*Urashima*) riding on it. Height, 2½ in. Side of square, 2¼ in.

> Porcelain. The base is decorated with waves in blue under the glaze. The tortoise is blue, the old man white. Same maker as No. 424.

No. 426.—Fire Holders, two. Height, 3½ in. Diameter 4¼ in.

> Covered with a rich chocolate-coloured glaze, on which are flowers, leaves, and butterflies in green, blue, pink, and yellow enamels. Mark, *Yaki nushi Sosendo*. Same maker as No. 424.

No. 427.—Water Vessel, with handle and spout. Height, 5 in.

> White porcelain, decorated with circular medallions of floral and leaf scrolls, delicately executed in green, blue, pink, red, and purple enamels. Made by Hansuke.

---

*This should have been included in Miscellaneous Specimens.—F. B.

No. 427A.—Cup. Diameter, 4¼ in. Depth, 3 in.

    Body glaze, cream-coloured and finely crackled. Decoration, a dragon in gold, in slight relief. A specimen of the ware made in Bishû to imitate Satsuma. Date, 1870.

KOTO WARE (PORCELAIN).

" This ware, also, is among the manufactures of the province of Omi. The factory was established near the eastern shore of Lake Biwa—the name Kotô signifies ' east of the lake '—about the year 1830. Its outcome from the first was porcelain decorated with blue under the glaze."

"It has a peculiar, soft, lustrous glaze. In some specimens this feature is so marked, that the surface of the ware looks as though oil had been rubbed over it."
—(*Vide* No. 428 of this Catalogue.)—From BRINKLEY's *History of Japanese Keramics*.

No. 428.—Sitting figure of Hotei, with bag. Height, 16 in. Width, 27 in.

    The face, breast, hands, and feet of figure are white; the drapery and bag, covered with diapers in blue under the glaze. Date, 1840. (The fan which Hotei carries is of Kyôtô porcelain. Date, 1850.)

No. 429. Rectangular Cake Box. Height, 5 in. Sides, 7½ in. x 4½ in.

    Decorated with figure and floral subjects in blue under the glaze. Date, 1840.

No. 430.—Cylindrical Flower Vase. Height, 9½ in. Diameter, 5 in.

    Round the base and rim are bands of diapers, on the body figure subjects and landscapes in red and gold. Date, 1850.

HIMEJI WARE (PORCELAIN).

"This ware was first produced about the year 1840, at the town of Himeji, in the province of Harima, the clay being obtained from a hill in the vicinity, called *Tozan*, whence the term *Tozan-yaki*. Himeji is the next post-town to Akashi on the Tokaido. The ware produced there was porcelain. The biscuit was not of first-class quality, but the decoration—blue under the glaze—was not only spirited in execution but often of pure and very brilliant tint. The productions of the kiln were formerly confined to small pieces, such as wine-bottles, tea-pots, water-vases, and so forth. In recent years the manufacture gradually ceased to be profitable, and the potteries are now no longer worked, but some of their output was very delicate and attractive."—From BRINKLEY'S *History of Japanese Keramics*.

No. 431.—Vase. Height, 5 in. Diameter, 3 in.
> Decorated with figure and floral designs in blue under the glaze. Date, 1840.

No. 432.—Wine Bottle, gourd-shaped. Height, 8½ in. Diameter, 3½ in.
> Decoration, houses and conventional clouds in blue under the glaze. Date, 1840.

MISCELLANEOUS.

No. 433.—Figure of Hotei, with bag. Height, 8 in. Width, 7 in.
> Stone-ware; *Shidoro-yaki*. Covered with brown glaze spotted with black. Date, 1770. (From the collection of Ninagawa Noritane.)

No. 434.—Tea Jar. Height, 3 in. Diameter, 2½ in.
> Faience. *Toyosuke Raku* ware. Covered inside with a greenish glaze; outside, with red lacquer, decorated with delicate diapers and medallions in gold, green, and black. Made by Toyosuke, at the Horaku factory in Nagoya.

No. 435.—Tea Cup. Diameter, 4 in. Depth, 3½ in.
> Faience. Covered with a greenish brown, speckled glaze, crackled. Round the rim is a band of chrysanthemums in white, inlaid. Mark, *Setosuke*. Date, 1640. (From the collection of Ninagawa Noritane.)

No. 436.—Gourd-shaped Vase. Height, 23 in. Diameter of lower lobe, 12 in.

> Faience *Soma* ware. The upper lobe is covered with black glaze, and decorated with a horse tied to a post in white *engobe*. The lower lobe is covered with a brown glaze run in globules. Date, 1770. (From the collection of Ninagawa Noritane).

No. 437.—Tea Jar. Height, 3 in. Diameter, 2¼ in. Kyôtô faience.

> Covered with a brown glaze run in very small, close globules, to imitate shark's skin (hence called *Same-yaki*), and decorated with stars in green and white *engobe*. Date, 1840.

No. 438.—Incense Box. Diameter, 2½ in. Depth, ½ in

> The bottom and inside of lid are covered with a black lacquer; the inside of body, with green glaze. Outside decoration, a green and gold design in relief among brown clouds. Faience. Made by *Kenya*, of Tôkyô.

No. 439.—Figure of Fukurokujin. Height, 5 in.

> The head is unglazed; the clothes are in red and black lacquer. Faience. Made by Ritsu-o of Kyôtô.

No. 440.—Figure of old Woman with Basket. Height, 8½ in.

> The face, arms, and legs unglazed; the rest of the piece covered with a light buff glaze, sparsely decorated with black. Faience. *Shigaraki* ware. Date, 1770.

No. 441.—Group of Seven Gods of Happiness, forming a votive piece. Height, 3½ in. Width, 4 in.

> Black clay, unglazed. *Imado* faience. Inscription on the bottom *An-yei gan-nen sho-gwatsu hoshi su* (reverentially offered up in the 1st month of the first year of Anyei, *i. e.*, 1772). Inscription on back *Tenka Taihei Kokka ansei Utokujin Kaiun shussei, Nikkwo*. This inscription is stamped inside a circle. It signifies:—"Offered to the fortune-giving God of Nikkwo as a supplication for peace and happiness, national and domestic, and personal fortune and advancement." Beside the circle are the characters *Benshi* (name of maker).

No. 442.—Figure of Genius Tekkai, seated on a Rock. Height, 12½ in.

> Covered with a honey-coloured glaze. *Minato* ware. Faience. Date, 1760.

No. 443.—Cup. Diameter, 3¼ in. Height, 3 in.

> The lower half inside is covered with a smooth cream-coloured glaze, crackled; the rest of the surface with a similar glaze run in globules. *Karatsu* ware. Faience. Date, 1670. (From the collection of Ninagawa Noritane.)

No. 444.—Cup. Diameter, 4½ in. Depth, 3¼ in.

    Covered with a dark-red glaze. *Agano* ware. Faience. Date, 1620. (From the collection of Ninagawa Noritane.)

No. 445.—Cup. Diameter, 3½ in.

    Body glaze, milk-white, crackled. Decoration in blue under the glaze; design, two figures under a tree watching a phœnix which flies toward them. *Odo* ware. Faience. Date, 1820.

No. 446.—Figure of old Man seated on a Rock. Height, 5½ in.

    Unglazed and intended to imitate a wood-carving. Pottery. Made by Hattori Tsuna, commonly called Korea, an artist of Tôkyô.

No. 447.—Figure of Genius, seated with a dragon coiled about his seat. Height, 7½ in.

    Covered with turquoise blue and purple glazes. Faience. Kobe ware. Modern.

No. 448.—Tea Pot. Height, 2½ in. Diameter, 3 in.

    Made in the shape of a lotus calix, the lid being a leaf. Faience. Unglazed outside; inside covered with a cream-coloured glaze crackled. Beside the handle are engraved the characters *Hachiju san Rengetsu*. (Made by Rengetsu, aged 83.) Rengetsu was a celebrated female artist of Kyôtô.

CHINESE PORCELAIN AND POTTERY.

'It is now a recognized fact that in China, and to a great degree in Japan, the art excellence of former times has sunk into a condition of marked decadence. Many causes have combined to bring about this result, but the most important, as well as the most comprehensive, is the loss of patronage. Patience that knew no weariness, and painstaking that kept no count of time, were distinguishing characteristics of the old artists, but they were characteristics which owed their development less to inspiration than to circumstance. In China, under successive Emperors from the Tang dynasty down to the middle of the seventeenth century, the Keramist's master-pieces were destined for Imperial use. He was able to be sure that whatever excellence he might obtain, at whatever cost, would be more than adequately appreciated ; and, since in those days there was but a small interval between divinity and royalty, ambition had a range beyond the measure of modern conception. Yet, even after so many long years of prosperous achievement—sufficient to have crystallized into a natural endowment the transmitted skill of fifty generations—a brief withdrawal of Court patronage had power to paralyze art. During the years that intervened between the fall of the Ming dynasty (1644) and the accession of the Emperor Kang-hi (1661), the outcome of the best factories scarcely deserved to be called mediocre ; and, again, although the reigns of that sovereign and his two successors are memorable as a period of *renaissance* culminating in hitherto unparalleled perfection, the illiberal policy of subsequent Emperors was the signal for an almost immediate loss of everything but tradition. Since the beginning of the present century, China has produced nothing that deserves to be classed for a moment with the works of her old masters. We miss altogether the depth and softness of color, fineness of paste, rich, velvety lustre of glaze, and brilliancy of enamels that distinguished, as they are infallible evidences of, her Keramic efforts prior to 1800. Nor does there seem to be any reasonable hope of an art revival. Whether, as some assert, the methods of former times have been lost, or whether desuetude has resulted in disability, the fact remains that in the present condition of Chinese art there is little to justify even the most sanguine patronage."—From BRINKLEY'S *History of Japanese Keramics*.

PLAIN WHITE.

No. 449.—Bowl, with very small base and wide rim. Diameter, 8 in. Depth, 2 in.

> Ivory white porcelain, very thin. On the inside is a scroll pattern engraved in the paste. *Yung-lo* period (1403-1425).

No. 450.—Bowl, with small base and wide rim. Diameter, 7 in. Depth, 2 in.

> Same ware and date as No. 449. Design, a rich floral scroll in relief. On the bottom is the character *To* (metropolis) which has evidently been cut in Japan.

No. 451.—Flower Vase, with narrow neck and swelling body. Height, 13½ in. Diameter, 8 in.

> White porcelain. Covered with an incised design of chrysanthemums and leaf scrolls. The vase has been made in two pieces and afterwards joined. Mark, *Tamin ching-hwa nien chi* (made in the period *Ching-hwa* of the Ming dynasty). Date, 1470.

No. 452.—Incense Burner, with three feet. Height, 10 in. Diameter, 6 in.

> Ivory white porcelain. Round the body is a band of key pattern and archaic designs incised. Date, 1500.

No. 453.—Bowl. Diameter, 7½ in. Depth, 4 in.

> White porcelain. The bottom, inside, and the whole of the outer surface are covered with an elaborate design of peonies and leaves in relief. Mark of the period *Kang-hi*, in blue. Date, 1665.

No. 454.—Flower Vase. Height, 18¼ in. Diameter, 8 in.

> White porcelain. Covered with floral and leaf scrolls, key patterns, &c., in high relief. Date, 1670.

No. 455.—Vase, with trumpet-shaped neck. Height, 18 in. Diameter of neck, 8½ in.

> White porcelain, covered with leaf scrolls, among which archaic dragons are entwined in relief. Mark, a leaf. Date, 1650.

No. 456.—Figure of Goddess Kwannon and Child. Height, 9½ in.

> Ivory white porcelain. Date, 1500.

No. 457.—Figure of Bunsho-sei (inventor of writing) standing on Marine Monster. Height, 8 in.

> White porcelain. Date, 1730.

No. 458.—Vase, square, with tapering neck and base. Height, 8½ in.

> White porcelain. Round the rim and shoulder are bands of key pattern and archaic designs in relief. On the sides are circular medallions of wave pattern, also in high relief. Mark of *Yung-ching* period in relief. Date, 1730.

No. 459.—Vase, with swelling body, tapering neck, narrow base, and four loop handles. Height, 8½ in. Diameter, 3¾ in.

> Ivory white porcelain. The body is ribbed. Mark of *Kien-lung* period, incised. Date, 1740.

No. 460.—Cups, five. Diameter, 5¾ in. Depth, 2 in.

> White porcelain. The body is pierced in a lace-work of exceeding delicacy. Date, 1600.

CRACKLED WARE.

No. 461.—Bowl, fluted so as to resemble a Chrysanthemum. Diameter, 8¼ in. Depth, 3¼ in.

> Faience. Covered with a buff-glaze, finely crackled. On the bottom inside is a flower incised. Date, 1520.

No. 462.—Vase, cylindrical, with tapering base and rounded shoulders. Height, 11 in. Diameter at shoulder, 3½ inches.

> Stone-ware. Covered with a cream-coloured glaze, very finely crackled. The crackles assume a circular shape, intended to resemble the roe of fishes. The space round the shoulders has no crackle. Date, 1560.

No. 463.—Vase, with swelling body and tapering neck. Height, 15½ in. Diameter of body, 6½ in.

> Same ware and period as No. 462, but the crackle is less clearly defined.

No. 464.—Vase, with swelling body and short neck. Height, 7½ in. Diameter, 6 in.

> Stone-ware. Cream-coloured glaze with exceedingly fine and regular crackle. Date, 1600.

No. 465.—Vase, square in section, with curved sides. Height, 10 in. Side, 7 in.

    Stone-ware. Rice-coloured glaze with bold crackle. Below the rim the crackle assumes the form of concentric circles, over the rest of the surface it runs in all directions. The crackle is of two sizes; the larger, black, and the smaller, brown. Round the lip is a band of key pattern incised. Date, 1470.

No. 466.—Tripod Incense Burner, with Elephant-head handles. Height, 7 in. Diameter, 12 in.

    White porcelain, boldly crackled. Round the body is a double line of key pattern. Date, 1650.

No. 467.—Vase, cylindrical, with tapering base. Height, 9 in. Diameter, 4 in.

    Stone-ware. Cream-coloured lustrous glaze, covered with a network of pink crackles. Date, 1730.

No. 468.—Fire box, circular. Diameter, $3\frac{1}{4}$ in. Height, $2\frac{1}{2}$ in.

    Stone-ware. Coloured with a lustrous, buff-coloured glaze, finely crackled Date, 1700.

No. 469.—Vase, with swelling body and trumpet-shaped neck. Height, 9 in. Diameter of neck, $6\frac{1}{2}$ in.

    Porcelain. A lustrous glaze of peculiar brownish white colour with bold crackle. Date, 1550.

No. 470.—Vase, with tapering body and long neck. Height, 14 in. Diameter of body, $7\frac{1}{2}$ in.

    Porcelain. A greenish white glaze with bold crackles in black and red. Date, 1780.

No. 471.—Vase, with swelling body and tapering neck. Height, 21 in. Diameter of body, 15 in.

    Porcelain A light green glaze, crackled. Mark of the *Kienlung* period in blue under the glaze. Date, 1760.

No. 472.—Vase, square above, with rounded body. Height, $17\frac{1}{2}$ in. Diameter of body, 8 in.

    Porcelain. Light green glaze with bold and clearly marked crackle. Mark of *Yung-ching* period in blue under the glaze. Date, 1730.

No. 473.—Vase, with tapering base and swelling shoulders. Height, $11\frac{1}{2}$ in. Diameter at shoulder, $6\frac{1}{2}$ in.

    Same ware, date and mark as No. 472, but a little darker.

No. 474.—Vase, with flattened sides and swelling body. Height, 4 in. Diameter of body, $2\frac{1}{2}$ in.

    A light green glaze, crackled. Date, 1680.

No. 475.—Bon-bon Holder. Height, 3½ in. Diameter, 3 in.
> Stone-ware. A brownish white glaze with red crackles. Date, 1760.

No. 476.—Tea Jar. Height, 2½ in. Diameter, 2¼ in.
> Stone-ware. A rich buff glaze with bold crackle. Date, 1650. (From the collection of Ninagawa Noritane.)

No. 477.—Incense Burner. Depth, 2 in. Diameter, 4½ in.
> Stone-ware. An exceedingly lustrous buff-coloured glaze, with bold crackle. Date, 1650.

No. 478.—Vase, with unglazed handles in form of lions' heads. Height, 7 in. Diameter, 4 in.
> Same ware, date and colour as No. 475.

No. 478A.—Vase. Height, 13 in. Diameter, 10 in.
> A greenish white glaze covered with a network of black and gray crackles. Date, 1760.

MONOCHROMATIC WARE.

CELADONS.

"Of Chinese wares, the oldest and one of the most valued is celadon, which is not, however, porcelain. It has hitherto been erroneously supposed, not only that the manufacture of porcelain proper in China was commenced at a very remote date, but also that a blue variety of great lustre and beauty was produced during the reign of the Emperor Chi-tsung (954). Chinese porcelain proper cannot boast any greater antiquity than about six centuries. Everything prior to the Yuen dynasty of Mongols (1260-1367) was either pottery or stone-ware. The eulogies of ancient authors apply to faience or glass, not porcelain, while, in point of colour, the much-talked of "blue" was not blue but green. The best Chinese and Japanese authorities are agreed that, when the Emperor Chi-tsung bade the Imperial Keramists study the hue of the "firmament as seen through the clouds after rain," he referred not to the azure overhead, but to the bluish green tints which, at such a time, are often seen near the horizon. His instructions were never completely carried out, perhaps, but certainly from his time, if not from an earlier period, the Chinese Keramist knew no higher aim than to produce a bluish green glaze of a velvet-like softness and delicate richness of colour that well justified the enthusiastic admiration of connoisseurs. Native amateurs attach the highest value to the oldest pieces of this ware, on the ground that the thick glazes employed up to the middle of the seventeenth century possess a finer lustre, and required a greater amount of technical skill on the potter's part, than their comparatively thin successors of the Kang-hi and Kien-lung Periods (1661-1795). Opinions may differ on this point, but it is at any rate certain that few really fine specimens of celadon find their way Westward at present, owing, in the first place, to their rarity; in the second, to the high estimation in which they are held by the native collectors."—From BRINKLEY'S *History of Japanese Keramics.*

No. 479.—Octagonal Vase, with swelling body and lion-head handles. Height, 14 in. Diameter, 4 in.

> Stone-ware, covered with a green glaze. The body is covered with sunken medallions containing designs in relief; those in the lower band of medallions being peonies and chrysanthemums; those in the middle band, storks and lotus plants, those in the shoulder band, the characters *Fok so tung hai, Siu pi lam san.* (May your good fortune be as deep as the Eastern sea, and may your life last as long as the Southern hills); those round the neck, flowers with the characters *T'ian bi-liok* (human happiness comes from heaven). Date, 1500.

No. 480.—Vase, with swelling body and trumpet-shaped neck. Height, 15 in. Diameter of body, 6½ in.

> Stone-ware, covered with a velvety, bluish-green glaze. The lower portion has two vertical bands of lotus leaves in relief; on the body is a scroll of flowers in high relief; the neck is ribbed. Date, 1400.

No. 481.—Vase, with tapering neck and ring handles. Height, 10¾ in. Diameter, 5½ in.

> Stone-ware, covered with a delicate bluish-green glaze. Date, 1400. (From the collection of Ninagawa Noritane.)

No. 482.—Vase, with tapering neck. Height, 10¾ in. Diameter, 5 in.

> Stone-ware, covered with an exceedingly beautiful green glaze. Date, 1400.

No. 483.—Gourd-shaped Vase. Height, 10½ in. Diameter of bottom lobe, 5½ in.

> Stone-ware, covered with a light green glaze, and having a scroll of peonies in relief running round each lobe. Date, 1430.

No. 484.—Bottle-shaped Vase. Height, 13¼ in. Diameter, 8 in.

    Stone-ware, covered with a delicate velvety green glaze. Date, 1430.

No. 485.—Vase, with tapering neck and large ring handles. Height, 12 in. Diameter, 6½ in.

    Stone-ware, covered with a warm green glaze. Round the base is a band of vertical lotus leaves in slight relief and round the neck a band of banana leaves incised. On the body are bunches of peonies and leaves in slight relief. Date, 1450.

No. 486.—Bottle-shaped Vase. Height, 13½ in. Diameter, 7 in.

    Stone-ware, covered with a warm green glaze. Round the neck are a vertical band of banana leaves and a band of key pattern, incised; round the base is a broad band of archaic design in relief; the body is covered with peony scrolls, also in relief. Date, 1450.

No. 487.—Vase, with swelling body and trumpet shaped neck. Height, 19 in. Diameter of body, 9 in.

    Stone-ware, covered with a warm green glaze. Round the base is a deep band of lotus leaves in relief; the upper part of the neck is ringed; the rest of the piece is covered with a scroll of leaves and flowers in relief. Date, 1450.

No. 488.—Cup. Diameter, 5 in. Depth, 2¼ in.

    Stone-ware, covered with a brownish green glaze. The outside is cut so as to simulate lotus leaves; the inside has an elaborate scroll of chrysanthemums and leaves. Date, 1400. This ware is known in Japan as *Shuko* celadon, because the colour was brought into vogue by the celebrated *Chajin*, Shuko, master of Tea Ceremonials to the Regent Yoshimasa (1480).

No. 489.—Tea Jar. Height, 2 in. Diameter, 2¾ in.

    Stone-ware, covered with a delicate green glaze, and having a floral design in relief. Date, 1450.

No. 490.—Bottle-shaped Vase. Height, 4½ in. Diameter, 3½ in.

    Stone-ware, covered with a rich green glaze, and having large metallic spots scattered over the surface. Date, 1500. This variety is the rarest and most valued in the East of all the celadons, and indeed of all Keramic productions.

No. 491.—Plate. Diameter, 6½ in.

    Stone-ware, covered with a warm green glaze. On the surface are two dragons in high relief, unglazed. Date, 1550.

No. 491A.—Bowl. Diameter, 10½ in. Depth, 5 in.

    Stone-ware. A warm green glaze with peonies and leaves incised. Date, 1550.

No. 492.—Vase, fluted, and with scalloped rim. Height, 5 in. Diameter, 3½ in.

> Porcelain, covered with a green glaze. On the faces are medallions with coiled dragons, fishes, and clouds in high relief. Date, 1580.

No. 493.—Incense Burner, in form of Dog of Fo. Height, 5 in. Length, 4 in.

> Stone-ware, covered with green glaze in which are metallic spots. On the head and body are nests of concentric circles cut in the *pâte*. Date, 1560.

No. 494.—Bowl. Diameter, 7½ in. Depth, 2½ in.

> Stone ware, covered with a green glaze, having a net-work of crackles in black and brown. Date, 1700.

No. 495.—Bowl. Diameter, 6 in. Depth, 3½ in.

> Porcelain, covered with a delicate green glaze. On the outside is a scroll of peonies and leaves incised. Date, 1680.

No. 496.—Plate. Diameter, 7 in.

> Stone-ware, covered with a delicate green glaze. The whole surface bears a beautifully executed design of leaf and floral scrolls, partly incised and partly in relief. Date, 1700.

No. 497.—Bowl. Diameter, 6 in. Depth, 3 in.

> Porcelain, covered with a light green glaze. The outside and bottom of inside are richly decorated with peonies and leaves in slight relief. Date, 1680. Mark, two peaches and leaves in blue under the glaze.

No. 498.—Vase, with swelling body and tapering neck and base. Height, 16½ in.

> Porcelain, covered with an exceedingly delicate light green glaze. Mark of the *Yung-ching* period. Date, 1725.

No. 499.—Vase, square in section, with swelling body and indented corners. Height, 14 in. Side, 7¼ in.

> Porcelain, covered with a light green glaze. The whole surface is ornamented with an exceedingly delicate lace-work of white designs (floral scrolls and archaic patterns) in slight relief. Mark of the *Kien-lung* period. Date, 1750.

No. 500.—Vase, with fluted body and scalloped rim and base. Height, 14¾ in. Diameter, 10 in.

> Porcelain, with a rich green glaze. Date, 1680.

No. 501.—Vase, with swelling body, narrow neck and base. Height, 13 in. Diameter of body, 10½ in.

> Porcelain, covered with a rich green glaze. Round the body is a broad band of archaic design in relief; round the base and neck, leaves and scrolls incised. Date, 1740.

No. 502.—Vase, with swelling body and narrow neck. Height, 13½ in. Diameter, 11 in.

> Porcelain, covered with a delicate green glaze. On the body are bats and clouds in slight relief. Round the neck and base are bands of key pattern, leaves, &c., partly in relief, partly incised. Date, 1740.

No. 503.—Vase, cylindrical, tapering above and below. Height, 16 in. Diameter, 7 in.

> Porcelain, covered with a warm green glaze. Round the lip and base are bands of leaves in slight relief; the rest of the surface is covered with a floral scroll, also in relief. Mark of *Ching-hwa* period (1465). Date, 1780.

No. 504.—Flower Vase, with cylindrical body and narrow neck. Height, 10 in. Diameter, 4 in.

> Porcelain, covered with a light green glaze. The whole body is decorated with a flower and leaf scroll in slight relief. Date, 1280.

No. 505.—Bowl. Diameter, 7 in. Depth, 3¾ in.

> Thick stone-ware covered with a muddy yellow glaze. Round the interior are figures and characters incised. On the bottom, inside, is a stag with the character *shika* (stag). Date, 1280. (From the collection of Ninagawa Noritane.)

No. 506.—Vase, with tapering neck and handles. Height, 10 in. Diameter, 5½ in.

> Stone-ware, covered with a greenish white glaze. On the body and round the neck and base are flowers, leaves, and archaic designs, some in high relief, others incised. Date, 1570. (From the collection of Ninagawa Noritane.)

No. 506A.—Incense Burner. Height, 3 in. Width across handles, 4½ in.

> Porcelain. A delicate buff glaze with designs in relief. Date, 1600. Silver Top.

MIRROR BLACK.

"Rarer and more valued than even the finest celadon is the mirror-black, with metallic spots or lines. The older varieties of this, date from the Sung and Yuen periods. They are stone-ware, and their marking is perhaps the most curious to be found in the whole range of the Chinese Keramist's productions. Of the same genus are the glazes known as 'Raven's-wing green,' 'Leveret-skin,' and so forth, all of which command such high prices and are so much sought after in the East that very few find their way into foreign collections."—From BRINKLEY's *History of Japanese Keramics.*

No. 507.—Jar-shaped Vase. Height, 7 in. Diameter, 5½ in.
    Heavy stone-ware, covered with a mirror black glaze shot with dark green. This colour is called in Japan *Usan*, or Raven's-wing black. Date, 1230.

No. 508.—Vase. Height, 7½ in. Diameter, 5 in.
    Stone-ware, covered with a mirror black glaze shot with violet. Date, 1400.

No. 509.—Vase, with tapering body and small neck. Height, 12 in. Diameter, 4 in.
    Porcelain, covered with a velvety mirror black dusted with very minute speckles of gold. Date, 1680.

No. 510.—Vase, with globular body, spreading neck and small base. Height, 8 in. Diameter, 7¼ in.
    Porcelain, covered with mirror black glaze dusted with gold speckles. Date, 1780.

No. 511.—Vase, elliptical in section, with swelling neck and ring handles. Height, 9¼ in.
    Porcelain, covered with an exceedingly lustrous light lilac glaze flecked with white. Date, 1680.

No. 512.—Vase, with tapering body and narrow neck and base. Height, 5½ in. Diameter, 2¼ in.
    Stone-ware, covered with a delicate lilac glaze running on the shoulder into a beautiful transparent blue. Date, 1630.

No. 513.—Vase, with globular body and trumpet-shaped neck. Height, 4 in. Diameter, 3½ in.
    Same ware and glaze as No. 512. Date, 1600.

No. 514.—Vase, with globular body and long, trumpet-shaped neck. Height, 16½ in. Diameter of body, 11 in.

    Same ware and glaze as No. 512. Date, 1680.

No. 515.—Egg-shaped Vase. Height, 6 in. Diameter, 4½ in.

    Stone-ware, covered with a lilac glaze, crackled. Date, 1700.

No. 516.—Vase, with swelling body and narrow neck. Height, 21 in. Diameter, 15 in.

    Porcelain, covered with a thin lilac glaze. The body is encircled by bands in relief. Date, 1650.

No. 516A.—Incense Burner, in the form of a Crab. Dimensions, 6 in. by 4 in.

    A brownish green glaze. Date, 1750. Stand of carved Red Lacquer.

No. 517.—Bowl, fluted. Diameter, 7½ in. Depth, 3½ in.

    Same ware, colour and date as No. 511.

No. 518.—Vase, for washing wine cups. Diameter, 5¼ in. Height, 4 in.

    Stone-ware, covered with a dark violet glaze. Date, 1700.

No. 519.—Vase, elliptical in section. Height, 13 in. Longer diameter, 9 in.

    Porcelain, covered with a light violet glaze. Date, 1750.

No. 520.—Vase, with swelling body and tapering neck. Height, 12½ in. Diameter, 9½ in.

    Porcelain, covered with a very light blue glaze. Round the shoulder is a band of key pattern and round the base a band of leaves, in relief. Date, 1740. Mark of *Kien-lung* period in blue under the glaze.

No. 521.—Vase, with swelling body and tapering neck. Height, 6½ in. Diameter, 4½ in.

    Porcelain, covered with a lustrous glaze of greenish blue. Date, 1700.

No. 522.—Vase, rectangular in section, with tapering neck. Height, 15 in. Sides, 8 in. and 6 in.

    porcelain, covered with a lustrous velvety dark blue glaze. Date, 1680.

No. 523.—Vase. Height, 20 in. Diameter, 9 in.

    Same ware, glaze and date as No. 522.

No. 524.—Vase, with swelling body, narrow neck and base. Height, 10 in. Diameter, 11 in.

> Same ware and glaze as No. 522, but the colour lighter. Date, 1700.

No. 525.—Vase, cylindrical, with tapering base and spreading neck. Height, 13½ in. Diameter, 7 in.

> Porcelain, covered with a lustrous indigo glaze. Date, 1780.

No. 526.—Figure of Daruma's Pupil, with shoe in his hand. Height, 9¼ in.

> Stone-ware, face, hands, and feet unglazed. Drapery covered with a bright indigo glaze. Date, 1780.

No. 527.—Bowl. Diameter, 6 in. Depth, 3 in.

> Porcelain, covered with a lustrous indigo glaze having a tinge of purple. Date, 1700.

No. 528.—Bowl and Saucer. Diameter of bowl, 4½ in. Height, 2¼ in. Diameter of saucer, 5½ in.

> Same ware, colour, and date as No. 527.

No. 529.—Vase, with swelling body and narrow neck. Height, 3¾ in. Diameter, 3¾ in.

> Porcelain, covered with an exceedingly lustrous deep indigo glaze. Date, 1720.

No. 530.—Vase, with swelling body. Height, 2½ in. Diameter, 2 in.

> Porcelain, covered with a lustrous lapis glaze. Date, 1700.

No. 531.—Tea-pot. Height, 2 in. Length, 5 in.

> Red *boccaro pâte* covered with a deep violet glaze. Date, 1680. Mark on the bottom *Beng-gwat it t'ian leong su sui* (a bright moon, a clear sky, and coolness like water). *Beng-sin* (name of maker). On the inside of lid *sui peng* (water level). (From the collection of Ninagawa Noritane.)

No. 532.—Bowl. Diameter, 7 in. Depth, 3 in.

> Porcelain, covered with a rich purple glaze. Date, 1680.

No. 533.—Stirrup Cup. Height, 4¾ in. Diameter, 6 in.

> Porcelain, covered outside with a light blue glaze. Round the inside are four medallions containing the characters in relief. *Kim-pong Te-beng* (name of maker). Between the medallions is a band of delicately cut floral scroll. Date, 1680.

No. 534.—Bowl. Diameter, 7 in. Depth, 3 in.

    Thin porcelain, covered with a lustrous canary yellow. On the bottom inside and round the outside dragons are incised in the paste. Mark of *Wan-leih* period (1573-1620), to which date the piece belongs.

No. 535.—Cup. Diameter, 4¼ in. Depth, 2¼ in.

    Porcelain; the inside white, the outside covered with a straw-yellow glaze, in which are incised dragons, clouds, and a band of archaic designs. Mark of *Kang-hi* period (1661-1722), to which date the piece belongs.

No. 536.—Cup and Saucer. Diameter of cup, 2 in. Height, 1½ in.

    Thin porcelain, covered with canary-yellow glaze. The centre of the saucer is raised to form a stand for the cup. Inside the raised portion is a leaf (mark) and round it a broad band of archaic designs incised. On the surface of the cup are leaves incised, and on the bottom the mark of the *Yung-lo* period (1403-1425). Date, 1760.

No. 537.—Bowl. Diameter, 6 in. Depth, 3 in.

    Porcelain, covered outside with a rich liver-coloured glaze; inside, white. Mark of *Kien-lung* period (1736-1795), to which date it belongs.

No. 538.—Plate. Diameter, 7½ in.

    Porcelain, covered with a peach-blossom-red glaze. Mark of *Shun-ti* period (1426-1436). Date, 1750.

No. 539.—Vase, with slender body and small neck. Height, 8½ in. Diameter, 4 in.

    Stone-ware, covered with a soft apple-green glaze slightly flecked and crackled. Date, 1660.

No. 540.—Incense Burner. Diameter, 5½ in. Depth, 2½ in.

    Pottery, covered with a bright apple-green glaze finely crackled. Date, 1800.

No. 541.—Vase. Height, 2½ in. Diameter, 1½ in.

    Stone-ware, covered with a dark apple-green glaze, crackled. Date, 1760.

No. 542. Pen Washer. Diameter, 2¼ in. Depth, ½ in.

    Stone-ware, covered with a dark apple-green glaze finely crackled. Inside is a crab in high relief and covered with a greenish black glaze. Date, 1800.

No. 543.—Libation Cup. Height, 4 in. Length, 5½ in.

    Pottery, covered with a lustrous dark green glaze. The outer surface is decorated with incised diapers, bands of key pattern, etc., after the fashion of bronze ornamentation. Date, 1790.

No. 544.—Ink-stand, in the shape of a leaf with Frog sitting on it. Length, 5 in. Width, 2¼ in.

    Porcelain, covered with a lustrous grass-green glaze. Date, 1760.

No. 545.—Egg-shaped Vase. Height, 6½ in. Diameter, 5 in.

    Stone-ware, covered with a light green glaze, beautifully crackled. Date, 1750.

No. 546.—Vase, gourd-shaped, with flattened sides. Height, 8¼ in. Diameter, 4½ in.

    Pottery, covered with a lustrous turquoise-blue glaze. Date, 1780.

No. 547.—Water Holder. Height, 3½ in. Length, 5½ in.

    Stone-ware, moulded so as to resemble the calix of a lotus, and covered with a greenish turquoise-blue glaze. The handle and spout are fabulous monsters. Date, 1800.

No. 548.—Vase, globular above, with tapering base. Height, 9 in. Diameter, 7 in.

    Heavy stone-ware, covered with a dark green glaze. Cochin-Chinese ware. Date, 900. (From the collection of Ninagawa Noritane.) The clay and glaze of this piece are identical with those of the tiles brought over from Cochin-China in the ninth century for the purpose of roofing a Japanese temple near Kyôtô.

No. 549.—Vase, with slender body, swelling waist, and spreading base.

    Heavy stone-ware, covered with a lustrous light green glaze. Cochin-Chinese ware. Date, 1400.

No. 550.—Vase, with Elephant-head handles. Height, 4½ in. Diameter, 4 in.

    Stone-ware, covered with a bluish gray glaze, crackled. Date, 1650.

No. 550A.—Vase, square. Height, 8 in. Side, 3½ in.

    A rich brown glaze, with dragons in relief on the side. Date, 1650.

No. 550B.—Bowl. Diameter, 6 in. Depth, 3 in.

    Porcelain. Apple-green glaze with incised designs. Mark of *Kang-hi* period. Date, 1680.

POLYCHROMATIC WARE.

"Another freak of the painstaking Celestial was to cover an olive-green or black glaze with a dust of yellow speckles; and to this class of work belongs a ware made to imitate patinated bronze, which is so much valued in China that the use of pieces without a blemish used to be confined to the Imperial family.

"Canary-yellow, aubergine-purple, apple-green, iron-red, ivory-white, *sang de bœuf*, *flambé*, and the like, need no comment. Genuine specimens commend themselves at once, and are so inimitable that the amateur is in no great danger of being misled. Of *sang de bœuf*, there are modern imitations without number, but their coarse paste and thin colour—a brick red—easily proclaim their inferiority. All these Chinese monochromes have been known and appreciated in Japan since the earliest days of their manufacture. But Japanese Keramists can scarcely be said to have seriously tried to imitate them. The almost insuperable difficulty of such an attempt was either realized from the first, or learned very soon by experience."—From BRINKLEY'S *History of Japanese Keramics*.

No. 551.—Vase, with swelling body and tapering neck. Height, 11½ in. Diameter, 7 in.

    Porcelain, covered with a dark olive green glaze, in which are mixed very fine speckles of yellow. Date, 1700.

No. 552.—Vase. Height, 7½ in. Diameter, 6 in.

    Porcelain, covered with an olive green glaze in which are mixed distinctly marked speckles of yellow. Mark of *Kien-lung* period. Date, 1750.

No. 553.—Stirrup Cup. Height, 4 in. Diameter, 6 in.

    Porcelain, covered with an olive green glaze in which are closely mixed very fine yellow speckles so that the piece has a distinctly yellow tinge. Date, 1650.

No. 554.—Vase, gourd-shaped, with narrow neck and large handles.

    Same ware and glaze as No. 553, but of a darker hue. Mark of *Kien-lung* period. Date, 1750.

No. 555.—Vase. Height, 2¼ in. Diameter, 1¾ in.

    Same ware, glaze, and date as No. 554, but having the yellow speckles less distinctly marked.

No. 556.—Vase. Height, 21 in. Diameter, 13½ in.

    Porcelain, covered with an olive green glaze, having distinctly marked yellow speckles. Date, 1730.

No. 557.—Vase. Height, 17½ in. Diameter, 10.

    Porcelain, covered with a very dark green speckled glaze to imitate patinated bronze. Round the body is a broad band of archaic designs and key pattern; round the neck a band of the character *Fuku* (wealth), the spaces being filled in with key pattern. On the shoulders and round the lower portions are circular medallions with the character *Ju* (congratulation). The designs are all in relief, and are intended to imitate the decoration on an old bronze. Date, 1700.

No. 558.—Incense Burner, with three legs. Height, 18 in. Diameter, 8½ in.

    Porcelain. A verdigris green glaze, in imitation of patinated bronze. On the body are fabulous animals and archaic dragons in relief. Round the rim are the characters *Kengsin lian siat-chi Tiansiong Seng-bo Te-tsu Li-yong-chun*. Made in the year *Keng-sin*, by the pupil *Li-yong-chun* (to burn incense before) the Queen of Heaven. Date, 1550. Massive Silver lid of delicate *repoussé* work.

No. 559.—Tea Jar. Height, 2¾ in. Diameter, 2 in.

    Porcelain. Olive green glaze, with yellow speckles. Date, 1800.

No. 560.—Vase, rectangular in section. Height, 6 in. Sides, 3½ in. × 3 in.

    Heavy stone-ware. Dark red glaze, flecked with purple. Date, 1650.

No. 561.—Jar. Height, 3½ in. Diameter, 4½ in.

    Stone-ware. Blood-red glaze, flecked with dark lines. Date, 1800.

No. 562.—Vase, with swelling body and long narrow neck. Height, 8 in. Diameter, 4¼ in.

    Stone-ware. Blood-red glaze, flecked with black and tinged with purple at the neck. Date, 1820.

No. 563.—Vase. Height, 11½ in. Diameter, 10 in.

    Stone-ware. Blood-red glaze, flecked with black and clouded with purple. Mark, on the bottom in blue under the glaze, illegible. Date, 1830.

No. 564.—Vase, square in section, tapering towards the base, with round neck. Height, 18 in. Side, 5½ in.

    Stone-ware. A lustrous glaze of blue, green, and brown tints. Date, 1700. Mark, *Ch'eng-hung-tong Chiu* (name of maker).

No. 565.—Vase, with lion-head handles. Height, 14 in. Diameter, 10 in.

    Stone-ware. Same glaze and tints as No. 564. Mark, *Koh Ming Tsiang-chi*. (Made by Koh Ming Tsiang.) The mark is forged. Date, 1780.

No. 566.—Water Holder, with handle and spout. Height, 8 in. Width, 9 in.

> *Boccaro* clay. A dark blue lustrous glaze, flecked with green. Mark same as that on No. 565, but genuine. Date, 1650.

No. 567.—Vase, Egg-shaped. Height, 9 in. Diameter, 6 in.

> Stone-ware. Dark blue glaze, flecked with green. Date, 1760.

No 568.—Vase, Egg-shaped. Height, 10¼ in. Diameter, 6½ in.

> Stone-ware. A mottled glaze of green and blue, the green largely predominating. Same mark as No. 565. Date, 1680.

No. 569.—Vase, Egg-shaped. Height, 9½ in. Diameter, 6¼ in.

> Stone-ware. Dark brown, flecked and spotted with blue. Date, 1680.

No. 570.—Vase. Height, 9 in. Diameter, 3½ in.

> Stone-ware. A very dark brown glaze, beautifully flecked with blue. Date, 1700.

No. 571.—Vase. Height, 9½ in. Diameter, 3½ in.

> Stone-ware. A blue glaze, beautifully mottled with white. Date, 1680.

No. 572.—Vase. Height, 11¼ in. Diameter, 4½ in.

> Stone-ware. A mottled light blue glaze, slightly flecked with purple. Date, 1680.

No. 573.—Vase. Height, 11 in. Diameter, 4 in.

> Stone-ware. A purplish glaze, beautifully flecked with blue and white. Date, 1650.

No. 574.—Vase. Height, 11 in. Diameter, 6 in.

> Stone-ware. Glaze, green, metallic red, blue, white, and black. Date, 1650.

No. 575.—Incense Burner, with three feet and handles. Height, 9 in. Diameter, 9 in.

> Stone-ware. A very beautiful glaze of skilfully blended green, blue, metallic red, and claret-colour. Date, 1700. Lid of *repoussé* bronze, with dragon and clouds in high relief.

No. 576.—Vase, Height, 8¼ in. Diameter, 6 in.

> Stone-ware. A lustrous black glaze, flecked and tinged with green, blue, and metallic red. Date, 1680.

No. 577.—Incense Burner, with three feet and handles. Height, 9½ in. Diameter, 9 in.

    Stone-ware. A delicate blue glaze, tinged with pink and flecked with white. Date, 1750. Lid cut in the shape of a lotus leaf, with carved Jade tip.

No. 578.—Vase. Height, 7 in. Diameter, 3 in.

    Stone-ware. A lustrous glaze of blue, green, white, metallic red, and claret-coloured tints. Date, 1750.

No. 579.—Dish, in the form of a leaf, with a spray of flowers at the stem. Length, 10½ in. Breadth, 7 in.

    Stone-ware. A lustrous blue glaze, flecked with white and passing into golden brown at salient points. Date, 1650.

No. 580.—Bowl, with scalloped edge and elliptical base. Height, 3 in. Diameter, 7 in. and 5 in.

    Stone-ware. A blue glaze, tinged with pink and spotted with black. Date, 1780.

No. 581.—Plate, with a scalloped edge. Diameter, 8 in.

    Same ware, glaze, and date as No. 579.

No. 582. Dish. Diameter, 10½ in. Depth, 2½ in.

    Porcelain. A peculiar grayish, green glaze, mottled with black and blue. Date, 1700.

No. 583.—Dish, in form of leaf. Length, 5 in. Breadth, 4½ in.

    Stone-ware. A rich brown glaze, flecked with blue and white and tinged with pink. Date, 1770.

No. 584.—Vase, with swelling shoulders and tapering base. Height, 10 in. Diameter, 4½ in.

    Stone-ware. A lustrous glaze, mottled with greenish white, claret-colour, and metallic red. Date, 1680.

No. 585.—Vase. Height, 6½ in. Diameter, 3½ in.

    Stone-ware. A lustrous, dark, claret-coloured glaze, flecked with blue and white at the shoulders, and with metallic red at the base. Date, 1720.

No. 586.—Vase. Height, 7 in. Diameter, 3 in.

    Stone-ware. A lustrous, creamy white glaze, flecked and mottled with metallic spots. Date, 1600.

No. 587.—Vase. Height, 7½ in. Diameter, 3½ in.

    Stone-ware. A greenish white glaze, flecked at the neck and base with metallic red. Date, 1700.

No. 588.—Vase. Height, 19 in. Diameter, 8¼ in.

>Porcelain. A light blue glaze, curiously flecked and spotted with black, and having large buff-coloured spots scattered over the surface. Date, 1688.

No. 589.—Tea Jar. Height, 3½ in. Diameter, 2½ in.

>Pottery, very fine *pâte*. Lustrous dark claret-coloured glaze, flecked with green and running into metallic brown at the edges. Date, 1600.

No. 590.—Tea Jar. Height, 2 in. Diameter, 1¾ in.

>Pottery. A lustrous brown glaze, flecked with blue. Date, 1600.

No. 591.—Libation Cup. Height, 3¼ in. Length, 4½ in.

>Faience. The glaze on the outer surface is a delicate blue, flecked with white and running into light pink at the edges; that on the inner surface is buff-coloured. Date, 1670.

No. 592.—Vase. Height, 4 in. Diameter, 2 in.

>Stone-ware. A brown glaze, flecked with blue. Date, 1800.

No. 593.—Pen Washer, in the form of half a peach kernel. Diameters, 5 in. and 3½ in.

>Pottery. The under surface is unglazed, but corrugated and stained so as to resemble the shell of a kernel. The inner surface is covered with a soft and very beautiful green glaze tinged with pink. Date, 1700.

No. 594.—Cup, with fabulous monster for handle. Length, 4½ in. Breadth, 3¼ in. Depth, 1½ in.

>Pottery. A soft lustrous green glaze run over a buff glaze. The outside has a scroll pattern and a band of diapers in relief showing buff-coloured through the green. Date, 1750.

No. 595.—Pen Washer. Height, 2 in. Length, 2 in.

>Same ware and glazes as No. 594. The outside is fluted, the flutes showing buff-colour through the glaze. Date, 1750.

No. 596.—Incense Burner, with three feet and handles. Height, 10½ in. Diameter, 9 in.

>Stone-ware. A pink glaze, flecked and spotted with green. Date, 1760. *Repoussé* Silver Top with *Howo* in high relief and an open-work pattern of clouds, beautifully executed.

No. 597.—Vase. Height, 6 in. Diameter, 2½ in.

>Faience. Turquoise blue glaze, flecked with purple. Date, 1830.

No. 598.—Pen Washer, in the form of a shell. Length, 2¼ in. Breadth, 2 in.

> Faience. Turquoise blue glaze, with metallic spots. Date, 1830.

No. 599.—Vase, in the form of the calix of a lily with tendrils. Height, 5 in. Diameter of neck, 3 in.

> Stone-ware. A thick, lustrous, buff-coloured glaze, with metallic spots. Date, 1680.

No. 600.—Vase. Height, 5½ in. Diameter, 3 in.

> Thin porcelain. A rich yellow glaze, with large liver-coloured spots. Date, 1760.

No. 601.—Vase. Height, 6½ in. Diameter, 3½ in.

> Porcelain. A variegated glaze of indigo and green. Date, 1800.

No. 602.—Vase, with Elephant-head handles. Height, 4 in. Diameter, 3 in.

> Same ware and glaze as No. 601, but lighter colours. Date, 1780.

No. 603.—Snuff Bottle. Height, 2¼ in. Diameter, 1½ in.

> Same ware, color, and date as No. 601.

No. 604.—Incense Burner. Height, 24 in. Diameter of top, 13¼ in.

> Faience. A light blue glaze. Round the base is coiled a dragon with purple scales, green belly, and yellow flames circling about it. The base and lobe above the dragon are pierced in a floral scroll. The top is pierced in a pattern of peonies and leaves in purple, green, and blue. Over this is a lion (*shishi*) in the act of leaping; his body is a light blue, and his mane and tail purple. The dragon and *shishi* are modelled with wonderful spirit. This piece was made by order of Funai, Duke of Izumo, in the year 1820. The design was sent from Japan.

No. 605.—Dish. Length, 8½ in. Width, 3½ in.

> Porcelain. A lilac glaze most curiously marked with white and blue lines (resembling crackle) under the glaze, which is thick and lustrous. N. B.—By what method this effect of spurious crackle has been produced, no explanation is offered by experts. Date, 1700.

No. 606.—Incense Burner. Height, 2½ in. Diameter, 3½ in.

> Stone-ware. A raven's wing black glaze. Date, 1760. Silver top, with open work *repoussé* design of chrysanthemum blossoms and leaves.

No. 607.—Incense Burner. Height, 2 in. Diameter, 3½ in.

> Porcelain. A very dark blue glaze with metallic brown edges and flecks. Date, 1720.

No. 608.—Incense Burner. Height, 7 in. Diameter, 6 in.

    Stone-ware. A lapis blue glaze, flecked with white to imitate the mineral. The lapis glaze is run over a green glaze which shows through in a few spots. Date, 1780.

No. 609.—Water Vessel. Depth, 3½ in. Length, 8 in.

    Faience. Covered inside with a deep lustrous green glaze, and outside with a rich yellow. The edges are purple, and round them is a double chain of chrysanthemum and plum blossoms and tassels. Date, 1750.

No. 610.—Vase. Height, 5½ in. Diameter, 2¾ in.

    Faience. Turquoise blue metallic spots and deep blue tints. Date, 1820.

No. 611.—Vase. Height, 8½ in. Diameter, 8½ in.

    Porcelain. A light red glaze, passing, in the lower half of the vase, into blue flecked with white. The inside has a bluish white glaze, and round the edge is a blue blush. Date, 1780.

No. 612.—Bon-bon Holder. Depth, 3½ in. Diameter, 3½ in.

    Faience. The lower portion is covered with a rich green glaze; the upper has various designs in slight relief, and is covered with a buff glaze, crackled. The band of design about the neck is picked out with red. Date, 1800.

No. 613.—Vase, gourd-shaped. Height, 8½ in. Diameter, 4 in.

    Stone-ware. A peach-coloured glaze, flecked with white, and divided into circular spaces by a skilfully run rich brown glaze. Date, 1750.

No. 614.—Vase. Height, 13 in. Diameter, 7½ in.

    Stone-ware. A rich variegated glaze of claret red, greenish brown, blue, and pinkish white, run together with considerable regularity. Date, 1739. Silver top.

No. 615.—Vase. Height, 7½ in. Diameter, 5½ in.

    Stone-ware. The vase has eight vertical flutes, down which run lines of rich blue glaze with white borders. Between the flutes the glaze is red flecked with blue. Mark of the period, *Kia-king*. Date, 1800.

No. 616.—Vase. Square. Height, 8 in. Side, 4 in.

    Stone-ware. A lustrous light blue glaze, run over a buff glaze, which shows through at salient points. The sides have the *Hakka* and *Swastika* in relief. Down the lower half of each side runs a patch of red. Date, 1800.

No. 617.—Bowl. Diameter, 7 in. Depth, 3 in.

    Stone-ware. A bluish glaze, running into green at the rim. Inside is a large blotch of blood red. Date, 1450.

No. 618.—Dish, in form of three pine leaves. Length, 8½ in. Breadth, 4 in.

>Stone-ware. Pink glaze, flecked with blue and white. Date, 1600.

No. 619.—Vase. Height, 8½ in. Diameter, 6½ in.

>Porcelain. A light lilac glaze, with a design of plum blossoms and bamboo leaves, in relief, appearing white under the glaze. Date, 1780.

No. 620.—Vase. Height, 15 in. Diameter, 9 in.

>Porcelain. A light mauve glaze, with designs in slight relief appearing white under the glaze. Date, 1760.

No. 621.—Incense Burner, with Silver Top. Height, 4½ in. Diameter, 3¾ in.

>Porcelain. A rich blue glaze curiously marbled and having characters in white (a verse of poetry relating to the four seasons) under the glaze. Mark of the *Ching-hwa* period. Date, 1650.

No. 622.—Vase. Height, 6½ in. Diameter, 6 in.

>Faience. A cream-white crackled glaze, with large metallic spots. Date, 1780.

No. 623.—Bowl. Diameter, 5 in. Depth, 2¾ in.

>Porcelain. A rich brown, with storks and lotus plants in white, in slight relief. Date, 1500.

No. 624—Water Holder. Height, 5 in. Diameter, 6 in.

>Faience. A light brown glaze, with large metallic spots. Date, 1760.

No. 625.—Incense Box. Diameter, 3 in. Depth, 1½ in.

>Porcelain. A mustard-yellow glaze. Round the base is a band of leaves and a key pattern in high relief. On the top is the character *Ju* (congratulation) in blue, in relief, and round it is a triple band of key pattern with archaic designs in green, blue and purple, in relief. Mark of *Kia-king* period. Date, 1800.

No. 626.—Tea Jar. Height, 3 in. Diameter, 2½ in.

>Porcelain. A mustard-yellow glaze, with a dragon in deep blue and flowers and leaves in purple and green. Date, 1780.

No. 627.—Plate. Diameter, 10¼ in.

>A canary-yellow glaze, with flowers in blue, reserved. Mark of *Hung-chi* period (1468–1506). Date, 1750.

No. 627A.—Vase, gourd-shaped. Height, 6 in. Diameter, 3½ in.

>A rich yellow glaze, with floral scrolls in blue, reserved. Mark of *Kea-tsing* period (1522). Date, 1700.

(123)

No. 628.—Tea Pot. Height, 3½ in. Width, 5 in.

>Stone-ware. The body is unglazed, but is divided by ribs of white glaze into six panels, containing landscapes in green and red enamels on a groundwork of diapers. All the designs are in relief. Date, 1720.

No. 629.—Vase. Height, 10 in. Diameter, 8 in.

>Faience. A grass-green glaze, with a yellow scroll of leaves and flowers in high relief. Cochin-Chinese ware Date, 1250. (From the collection of Ninagawa Noritane.) N. B.—The facsimile of this piece is depicted in Jacquemart's work as Korean.

No. 630.—Vase. Height, 10½ in. Diameter, 8 in.

>Faience. A brown glaze finely crackled and clouded with blue Cochin-Chinese ware. Date, 1300.

No. 631.—Tripod Incense Burner, with Silver Inlaid Top. Height, 4 in. Diameter, 3½ in.

>Porcelain. A dark blue glaze covered with small metallic spots. Date, 1650.

No. 632.—Vase, rectangular in section, with swelling body. Height, 9 in. Sides, 4 in. and 3 in.

>Porcelain. Iron-red glaze, with strongly marked metallic lines and spots. The inside and bottom are covered with white glaze. Date, 1600.

No. 633.—Vase, with trumpet-shaped neck. Height, 13½ in. Diameter, 9 in.

>Porcelain. An iron-red glaze covered with very fine metallic spots. Date, 1680.

No. 634.—Vase, with swelling body and tapering neck and base. Height, 7¼ in. Diameter, 3 in.

>Porcelain. A dead-leaf glaze, with dark metallic spots. Date, 1700.

No. 635.—Bowl. Diameter, 5¼ in. Depth, 2½ in.

>Porcelain. Iron-red glaze, with bright metallic lines. Date, 1650.

No. 636.—Tea Jar, egg-shaped. Height, 3 in. Diameter, 2¼ in.

>Porcelain. Iron-red glaze, with metallic lines and spots. Date, 1650.

No. 637.—Tea Jar, egg-shaped. Height, 2¾ in. Diameter, 1¾ in.

>Same ware, date and colour as No. 636, but having the metallic spots finer and closer.

No. 638.—Vase. Height, 4 in. Diameter, 1¾ in.

    Porcelain. A lustrous red glaze, with fine metallic spots. Date, 1700.

No. 639.—Incense Burner, with open-work Silver Top. Height, 3½ in. Diameter, 4 in.

    Same ware, colour and date as No. 638, but having fewer metallic spots.

No. 640.—Vase, with Silver Top. Height, 6 in. Diameter, 5½ in.

    Porcelain. Metallic brown glaze, with floral designs in white, in relief. Date, 1650.

No. 641.—Incense Burner in the form of a Tiger. Height, 2 in.

    Porcelain. A white glaze, streaked with red and black to represent the tiger's hair. Date, 1650. (From the collection of Ninagawa Noritane.)

No. 642.—Vase. Height, 14½ in. Diameter, 6 in.

    Porcelain. A light blue glaze, beautifully veined. The handles are unglazed lion's heads delicately modelled. Date, 1600.

No. 643.—Vase, with swelling body and slender trumpet-shaped neck. Height, 27½ in. Diameter, 10½ in.

    Porcelain. A blue glaze, clouded and flecked. Date, 1600.

No. 644.—Plate. Diameter, 16½ in.

    Porcelain. A slate-blue glaze, with a design of three *shishi*, a ball, and streamers in lilac and black, in relief. Date, 1830.

No. 645.—Cups, five. Diameter, 3½ in. Depth, 2 in.

    Porcelain. An exceedingly rich blue *soufflé* glaze. Date, 1700.

No. 646.—Vase. Height, 7½ in. Diameter, 4½ in.

    Porcelain. Slate-blue glaze, with a bunch of lotus leaves and flowers in lilac, green, and white. Date, 1830.

No. 647.—Cup. Diameter, 4 in. Depth, 3 in.

    Dark stone-ware. Round the rim is a band of green glaze. On the body are pine-trees, clouds, a stork, and a verse of poetry in white, blue, and brown enamels in relief. On the side are the characters *Chiku-ten-ro* (name of kiln), and on the bottom the mark of the *Wanleih* period. Date, 1575.

No. 647A.—Vase. Height, 14 in. Diameter, 7 in.

    Stone-ware. A rich brown glaze, flecked with blue and white. Date, 1800.

No. 647B.—Incense Burner. Height, 4½ in. Diameter, 6 in.

A dead-leaf brown glaze, slightly mottled, with a band of claret colour round the rim. Date, 1650. Silver top.

KIEN-YO WARE.

"The *Kien-yô*, called in Japan *Temmoku* or *Kenzan*, was a ware which had no peer in point of technical excellence. It owed its production to the demand of tea-drinkers. Under the Tang dynasty (618–907), tea became an article of common consumption in China, and its popularity thenceforth increased so rapidly that a subsequent exponent of its reputation under the Sung rulers (960–1279) ascribed to it seven imcomparable properties; namely, assuaging thirst, promoting digestion, clearing the throat, dispelling drowsiness, stimulating the kidneys, raising the spirits, and refreshing fatigue. Chinese society lived a life too colourless and unpoetical to suggest anything like the graceful, idealistic philosophy of the Japanese *Cha no Yu*. But Chinese tea-drinkers soon formed a clear conception of the qualities a tea-bowl should possess in order to render the beverage as grateful as possible both to eye and palate. These qualities the *Kien-yô* exhibited in the highest degree. Thick enough to prevent the tea from cooling rapidly, its *pâte* was of such a nature as not to convey the heat of the beverage to the drinker's hand or lips, while its glaze not only offered a pleasant contrast to the bright green of the powdered tea, but was also admirable for its own sake. In truth, the glaze of the *Kien-yô* was a marvel. On a ground of mirror-black we find shifting tints of purple and blue; reflections of deep green, like the glassy colour of the raven's wing; lines of soft silver, regular as the fur of the leveret (hence known in China as *Tō-hō-yō*, or "hare's-fur ware") and sometimes, in specimens of later date, the decoration takes the form of conventional Phœnixes (*Ho-wo*), butterflies, maple-leaves, and so forth, in golden brown of the greatest richness and beauty. All these designs and tints possess the same property as that described in the case of spotted celadon—they seem to float in the glaze In short, the *Kien-yô*, though its *pâte* scarcely deserves to be called stone-ware, must be ranked, for the sake of its glaze, as a triumph of Keramic skill. The most dexterous workmen of modern times have completely failed to imitate it, and authentic specimens are as rare as they are unmistakable. During the past five centuries, cups of this ware have been almost indispensable to the Japanese *chajin*. Before the nation turned, fourteen years ago, from its life of luxurious refinement, a single specimen of the best varieties commanded a price of from fifteen hundred to two thousand dollars"—From BRINKLEY'S *History of Japanese Keramics*.

[The pieces enumerated below were collected with much difficulty and during a number of years. They have all been examined by the best experts in Japan, and the descriptions here given are probably quite trustworthy.]

No. 648.—Cup, with Silver rim. Diameter, 5 in. Depth, 2½ in.

    Heavy stone-ware. Lustrous black glaze, having purple and blue tints and regularly marked fine metallic lines. Date, 1125. (From the collection of Ninagawa Noritane.) Stand of Black and Gold Lacquer.

No. 649.—Cup, with Silver rim. Diameter, 5 in. Depth, 3 in.

    Same ware and date as No. 648, but the glaze is a glossier black and the metallic lines are better marked. Stand of Black and Gold Lacquer.

No. 650.—Cup, with Silver rim. Diameter, 4½ in. Depth, 2½ in.

    Heavy stone-ware. Hare-skin glaze. Date, 1200. (From the collection of Ninagawa Noritane.) Black and Gold Lacquer Stand.

No. 651.—Cup, with Silver rim. Diameter, 5¾ in. Depth, 2½ in.

    Heavy stone-ware. A glossy black glaze, covered with fine and perfectly regular metallic lines. Date, 1180. Mark illegible. Stand of Carved Red Lacquer.

No. 652.—Cup, with Copper rim. Diameter, 7 in. Depth, 3 in.

    Same ware, glaze, and date as No. 651, except that the metallic lines are more numerous. (Broken slightly at the rim and repaired with gold.) Red Lacquer Stand.

No. 653.—Cup, with Silver rim. Diameter, 6½ in. Depth, 2¾ in.

    Heavy stone-ware. A glossy black glaze, covered with small, clearly marked metallic spots. Date, 1180. Gold Lacquer Stand.

No. 654.—Cup. Diameter, 6 in. Depth, 2 in.

    Fine stone-ware. A lustrous black glaze, covered with large spots of peculiar yellow colour, with a pink and blue bloom. Date, 1350. Gold Lacquer Stand.

No. 655.—Cup. Diameter, 4½ in. Depth, 2 in.

    Heavy stone-ware. On the inside a finely veined brown glaze, with a tinge of blue and red, and having design of two claret-coloured *Howo*, incorporated in the glaze. The outside is a dark claret colour, with bluish white spots and streaks. Date, 1300. Gold Lacquer Stand. (The glaze of this piece has lost nearly all lustre from use.)

No. 656.—Cup. Diameter, 5 in. Depth, 2½ in.

    Red stone-ware. Covered with a rich brown glaze, over which is run, on the inside, a greenish white glaze with blue flecks, the brown glaze showing through in a pattern of stars. Date, 1400. Black and Gold Lacquer Stand.

PORCELAIN, PAINTED WITH BLUE UNDER THE GLAZE.

"Next to celadon, and omitting a few other rare varieties, 'blue and white' is most highly esteemed in the countries of its production.

"And here it may be mentioned that fineness of paste and lustre of glaze are the only infallible criteria of age, in porcelain and pottery alike. The workmen of former times evidently prepared their materials by processes which are beyond either the ability or the patience of their degenerate successors."—From BRINKLEY'S *History of Japanese Keramics*.

No. 657.—Fire Holder. Diameter, 4½ in. Depth, 2½ in.

    A yellowish white glaze, with a roughly executed design, in dark blue, of a castle and various circles, spirals, &c. Date, 1200. This specimen shows the earliest attempts of the Chinese to produce porcelain. (From the collection of Ninagawa Noritane.)

No. 658.—Plates, three, with scalloped edges. Diameter, 8 in.

    The centres of the plates have floral designs with birds and insects. Round the rim is a band of floral scroll with rabbits scattered through it. Date, 1400.

No. 659.—Bowl. Diameter, 12 in. Depth, 4 in.

    The outside is sparsely decorated with archaic scrolls. The inside has a ground work of diapers among which are medallions with floral designs, scrolls, and tassels. The bottom has clay adhering to it. Date, 1300.

No. 660.—Bowl. Diameter, 8½ in. Depth, 3 in.

    Covered inside and outside with branches of trees and shrubs. Mark of *Shun-ti* period (1426-1436) to which it belongs. (From the collection of Ninagawa Noritane.)

No. 661.—Stirrup Cups, five. Height, 4 in. Diameter, 3¾ in.

    Design, fishes, dragons, and fabulous monsters in white among conventional blue waves and clouds. On the stem, two rabbits in white on a blue ground. Mark and date, *Shun-ti* period (1426-1436).

No. 662.—Water Vessel, with spout and handle. Height, 12½ in. Diameter, 7½ in.

    The spout and handle are decorated with floral scrolls, the body and lid with five-clawed dragons in circles and bands. Mark and date, *Lung-king* period (1567-1674).

No. 663.—Water Vessel, with spout and handle. Height, 4½ in. Diameter, 4 in.

    The sides have panels of open work, between which and round the shoulder are floral scrolls. The lid is also perforated. Date, 1550. (From the collection of Ninawaga Noritane.)

No. 664.—Vase. Height, 11½ in. Diameter, 9 in.

    Round the neck and base are bands of floral scrolls. The body is decorated with storks flying upwards from rocks overgrown by conventional plants. Round the shoulder are four characters signifying "Peace to the country and happiness to the people." Mark and date, *Wan-leih* period (1573-1620).

No. 665.—Rectangular Box. Sides, 11 in. and 8 in. Depth, 4 in.

    Decorated inside with flowers and trees, outside with figure and floral subjects. Mark and date, *Wan-leih* period (1573-1620).

No. 666.—Incense Box. Height, 2½ in. Diameter, 3 in.

    Decoration, floral sprays. Mark and date, *Kea tsing* period (1522-1667).

No. 667.—Bowl. Diameter, 7½ in. Depth, 3 in.

    Thin porcelain. Decoration, five-clawed dragons and lotus leaves. Mark and date, *Wan-leih* period (1573-1620).

No. 668.—Shallow Bowl. Diameter, 5 in. Depth, 2 in.

    Thin porcelain. Decoration, five-clawed dragons and flames. Mark and date, *Wan-leih* period (1573-1620).

No. 669.—Tea Jar. Height, 2 in. Diameter, 2 in.

    Decoration, five-clawed dragons, waves and flames. Date, 1600.

No. 670.—Tripod Incense Burner, upper part in the form of a melon. Height, 5 in. Diameter, 4½ in.

> The lower portion is covered with diapers. The upper, has three circles of open work between which are conventional clouds. Date, 1650. Mark, *Sui-nan chi-chi* (carefully made by Sui-nan).

No. 671.—Bowl. Diameter, 5½ in. Depth, 2 in.

> Decoration on the outside pines, plums, and bamboos; on the inside, storks and flames, with a rabbit under a tree on the bottom. Mark signifying masterpiece of *Kin-tang*. Date, 1550. (This variety of blue and white porcelain is most highly esteemed in Japan).

No. 672.—Jar, with lotus leaf cover. Height, 11½ in. Diameter, 13 in.

> Round the shoulder is a floral scroll. The body is decorated with figure subjects. Date, 1550.

No. 673.—Vase, in the form of a pilgrim's bottle. Height, 14½ in. Diameter, 11 in.

> Round the neck and base are bands of leaves. On the body is a plum tree with birds. Date, 1650.

No. 674.—Bowl. Diameter, 8 in. Depth, 3 in.

> The inside plain; the outside decorated with figure subjects. Mark of *Shun-ti* period (1426). Date, 1650.

No. 675.—Cup, with silver rim. Diameter, 5 in. Depth, 2½ in.

> On the bottom inside is a landscape. Round the rim and base outside are bands of diaper. On the body are six circular medallions with landscapes; the space between which is occupied by a key-pattern diaper, in relief, forming a network of glaze through which the unglazed *pâte* is visible. Mark of *Wan-leih* period (1573). Date, 1650.

No. 676.—Box, in the form of two diamonds. Length, 7 in. Width, 3 in.

> The top is decorated with five-clawed dragons: the rest of the surface with floral sprays and insects. Mark and date, *Wan-leih* period (1573-1620).

No. 677.—Water Vessel, with spout and handle. Height, 7½ in. Width, 8½ in.

> On the sides are large medallions containing five-clawed dragons, flames, etc. The rest of the surface has storks, leaves, etc. Mark and date, *Wan-leih* period (1573-1620).

No. 678.—Cup. Diameter, 3½ in. Depth, 2 in.

    The inside is plain. Round the rim and base, outside, are bands of diaper. Round the body are six circular medallions with floral subjects, the space between them being perforated in a delicate design of interlacing circles. Mark of *Shun-ti* period (1426). Date, 1650.

No. 679.—Cup, with silver rim and pewter base. Diameter, 3¾ in. Depth, 2 in.

    The inside is plain. Round the rim and base, outside, are bands of diaper. Round the body are nine figures, the space between which is perforated in a delicate design of interlacing circles. Date, 1650.

No. 680.—Incense Burner. Height, 2½ in. Diameter, 3 in.

    The top is pierced in a delicate design of interlacing circles, among which is a chrysanthemum scroll in relief. Round this is a band of conventional dragons. The body is decorated with floral subjects and insects. Mark of *Yung-lo* period (1433). Date, 1639.

No. 681.—Bowl. Diameter, 8 in. Depth, 4 in.

    Inside plain. Outside, a delicately executed design of children at play, trees, and flowers. Date, 1680.

No. 682.—Bowl. Diameter, 8 in. Depth, 4 in.

    On the bottom, inside, a *Kirin*. Outside, children at play, houses, trees, &c., in very dark blue. Date, 1660.

No. 683.—Trumpet-shaped Vase. Height, 17½ in.

    Decoration, floral subjects, rocks, birds, and a band of leaves. Date, 1870.

No. 684.—Vase, cylindrical. Height, 18 in. Diameter, 6 in.

    Decoration, figures, plantain trees, rocks, &c. Date, 1650.

No. 685. Vase, cylindrical. Height, 16 in. Diameter, 5 in.

    Decoration, women, children, plantain trees, rocks, &c. Date, 1650.

No. 686.—Vase, with swelling shoulders, small neck, and tapering base.

    Archaic decoration, partly blue on a white ground and partly white on a blue ground. Date, 1670.

No. 687.—Vase, trumpet-shaped. Height, 8 in. Diameter, 5 in.

    Round the rim is a band of incised scroll pattern; round the centre are two bands of incised diapers, between which is a band of blue scrolls. The upper part is decorated with floral subjects and insects. Round the base is a band of leaves. Date, 1680.

(131)

No. 688.—Vase, trumpet-shaped. Height, 8 in. Diameter, 3½ in.

    Decoration, bamboos, peonies, a bird, and an insect. Date, 1680.

No. 689.—Vase, cylindrical. Height, 10½ in. Diameter, 3½ in.

    Decoration, figure subjects, trees, rocks, &c. Round the shoulders and base are bands of incised diapers. Date, 1680.

No. 690.—Vase, with globular body and long neck.

    The body is decorated with scrolls; the neck has a band of key-pattern and plantain leaves. Mark and date, *Kien-lung* period (1736-1795).

No. 691.—Ginger Jar, with Black-wood lid inlaid with Silver and carved Jade knob. Height, 8½ in. Diameter, 7 in.

    Hawthorne pattern. Date, 1680.

No. 692.—Gourd-shaped Jar, with Black-wood lid inlaid with Silver and carved Jade knob. Height, 8½ in. Diameter, 7 in.

    Rich blue *soufflé* glaze with a flight of storks in white. On the bottom is the following inscription : *Taisei Kenriu shijiu nen haru sangwatsu kibo Kosei Keitokuchiu Inyeido Nihon koku Nioi-an no motome ni ojite tsukuru.* Made by Inyeido at the Keitoku office in Kosei, by request of the Japanese Nioi-an, on the 15th of the 3rd month of the 40th year of *Kien-lung* (1776).

No. 693.—Vase, with globular body and long neck. Height, 10½ in. Diameter, 4½ in.

    Decoration, flowers and butterflies. Date, 1700.

No. 694.—Tea Jar. Height, 2½ in. Diameter, 2 in.

    Decoration, floral scrolls. Mark of *Shun-ti* period (1426). Date, 1750.

No. 695.—Vase. Height, 4½ in. Diameter, 2½ in.

    Decoration, floral scrolls and bands of diaper. Date, 1750.

No. 696.—Tea Jar. Height, 2 in. Diameter, 2 in.

    Decoration, floral scrolls. Mark of *Kea-tsing* period (1522). Date, 1750.

No. 697.—Plate. Diameter, 7¼ in.

    Body glaze, a rich lapis blue, marbled. On the bottom inside and round the edge outside are fishes and lotus plants in white. Mark of *Shun-ti* period (1426). Date, 1700.

No. 698.—Vase. Height, 4½ in. Diameter, 2 in.
> Decoration, floral scrolls and plantain leaves. Mark of *Shun-ti* period (1426). Date, 1770.

No. 699.—Bon-bon Holder. Height, 4½ in. Diameter, 2 in.
> Decoration, floral scrolls. Mark of *Kea-tsing* period (1522). Date, 1750.

No. 700.—Vase. Height, 4½ in. Diameter, 3 in.
> Round the body are bands of plantain leaves and conventional designs: round the shoulder is a band of floral scroll. Date, 1700.

No. 701.—Vase. Height, 3 in. Diameter, 1½ in.
> Decoration, floral scrolls and a band of plantain leaves. Mark of *Shun-ti* period (1426). Date, 1750.

No. 701A.—Vase, trumpet-shaped. Height, 7 in. Diameter, 5½ in.
> Decoration similar to that of No. 687. Date, 1680.

No. 702.—Bowl, octagonal with fluted angles. Diameter, 8¼ in. Depth, 4 in.
> The outside is decorated in eight panels containing figure subjects; the blue colour being curiously laid on so as to appear, in part, dark, and, in part, exceedingly light. Round the rim inside is a band of diapers with reserved designs. Mark of *Ching-hwa* period.(1465). Date, 1750.

No. 703.—Incense Box. Diameter, 3½ in. Depth, 1½ in.
> Decoration, a very delicately executed design of 65 children at play. Mark of *Ching-hwa* period (1465). Date, 1720.

No. 704.—Incense Box. Diameter, 3 in. Depth, 1½ in.
> Decoration, floral scrolls in white on a rich blue ground. Mark of *Wan-leih* period (1573). Date, 1750.

No. 705.—Stirrup Cup. Height, 4 in. Diameter, 4 in.
> Design, floral scrolls and a band of cords and tassels. Mark and date, *Kien-lung* period (1736-1795).

No. 706.—Water Vessel. Height, 6½ in. Diameter, 2 in.
> Decoration, figure subjects and landscapes, Date, 1700.

No. 707.—Cup with Lid. Height, 3½ in. Diameter, 4 in.
> Decoration, a network of blue lines among which are plum blossoms whose petals have been cut out and filled in with green glaze so as to be transparent. Mark, *Chu-tong tsang-gwan* (Precious toy of the Chu Hall). Date, 1750.

No. 708.—Tripod Incense Burner, with elephant-head handles and feet.

> Decoration, a landscape. Date, 1700.

No. 709.—Incense Box, in the form of a coiled dragon.

> The dragon is blue, the ground white. Date, 1820.

No. 710.—Incense Burner. Height, 2½ in. Diameter, 2½ in.

> Decoration, insects, flowers and floral scrolls. Date, 1550.

No. 711.—Incense Box, in the shape of an egg plant. Length, 2¼ in. Height, 1¼ in.

> Decoration, a diaper of deep blue bands, among which are white plum petals. Mark and date, *Kien-lung* period (1736–1795).

No. 712.—Incense Box, in the shape of a peach with spray and flowers in high relief. Diameter, 2 in. Height, 1½ in.

> Decoration, a band of blue diaper. Date, 1800.

No. 713.—Incense Box. Diameter, 2½ in. Depth, 1 in.

> Decoration, children at play and a landscape. Mark of *Ching-hwa* period (1465). Date, 1750.

No. 714.—Incense Box, in the form of a dog sitting. Height, 2½ in.

> Covered with a deep blue glaze, except the breast, nose, &c., which are white. On the body are white stars. Date, 1820.

No. 715.—Bowl, with Cover. Diameter, 7 in. Height, 5½ in.

> Covered with a floral scroll among which are dragons and phœnixes. Mark and date, *Yung ching* period (1723–1736).

No. 716.—Ginger Jar, with Black-wood Top, inlaid with Silver and having Jade tip. Height, 8 in. Diameter, 9 in.

> The ground is Hawthorn pattern, among which are circular medallions, with floral designs. Date, 1830.

No. 717.—Eight Cups. Viz.:—

> No. 1. Porcelain decorated with a delicately executed landscape in blue under the glaze. Diameter, 3¼ in. Height, 3½ in. Mark of *Shun-ti* period (1526). Date, 1670.
> No. 2. Porcelain decorated with a floral scroll in deep blue under the glaze. Diameter, 3 in. Depth, 1¾ in. Mark of *Wan leih* period (1575). Date, 1740.
> No. 3. Porcelain covered with a cream white glaze, crackled. Diameter, 3¼ in. Depth, 2 in. , Mark *Ko* (old).
> No. 4. Porcelain decorated with dragons and floral scrolls in red, green, and yellow over the glaze. Diameter, 3¼ in. Depth, 1¾ in. Mark of *Wan-leih* period (1573). Date, 1750.
> No. 5. Thin porcelain, decorated with plums, bamboos, and birds in blue under the glaze. Diameter, 2 in. Depth, 1½ in. Mark of *Ching-hwa* period (1465). Date, 1750.
> No. 6. Porcelain, decorated with conventional symbols, leaves, insects, and a band of diaper in blue under the glaze. Diameter, 3¾ in. Depth, 1¼ in. Mark of *Wan-leih* period (1573). Date, 1700.
> No. 7 The fac-simile of No. 3.
> No. 8. Thin porcelain, decorated with cocks, hens, chickens, and floral designs in blue under the glaze. Diameter, 2½ in. Depth, 2 in. Mark. *Hi-tso ki-gwan chi chiu*. (Precious and rare toy *for use* at sunrise.) Date, 1700.

PORCELAIN, PAINTED WITH VARIOUS COLOURS UNDER THE GLAZE.

No. 718.—Plate. Diameter, 8 in.

> Round the edge, outside, are eight Genii riding upon fishes, leaves, fabulous animals, &c., among conventional waves. The figures are blue; the waves, red. On the bottom, inside, are figures of Fukuroku-jin and stag, in blue, among red waves. Mark, *Chai-siu-tong-chi*. (Made at the Hall of excellent painting.) Date, 1700.

No. 719.—Plate. Diameter, 6½ in.

> Design and colouring, the fac-simile of No. 718. Mark, *Yok-hian Su-ok*. (Hall of diligent painting.) Date, 1700.

No. 720.—Snuff Bottle. Height, 3 in. Diameter, 1 in.

> Design, eight men on horseback approaching a castle gate in which a man stands with folded arms. Mark and date, *Shun-chi* period (1644-1661).

No. 721.—Vase. Height, 3½ in. Diameter, 1½ in.
> Curiously marbled with red and blue. Date, 1750.

No. 722.—Bowl. Diameter, 8 in. Depth, 4 in.
> Round the rim, inside and outside, is a band of key pattern; the rest of the surface is covered with a bold floral scroll. The decoration is entirely in red. Date, 1780.

No. 723.—Vase. Height, 11 in. Diameter, 8 in.
> Design, dragons and floral scrolls in red. Date, 1750.

No. 724.—Vase. Height, 18½ in. Diameter, 8 in.
> Decorated with horses, trees, and rocks in blue, liver-colour, and black under the glaze. Date, 1820.

No. 725.—Vase. Height, 9 in. Diameter, 3½ in.
> A mustard-yellow glaze, with a design of flowers and leaves in dark brown. Date, 1800.

No. 726.—Pen Holder, cylindrical. Height, 4½ in. Diameter, 2½ in.
> Decoration, a dragon, clouds, and flames in light green. The design is incised. Mark, and date, *Kien-lung* period (1735-1796).

No. 727.—Bowl. Diameter, 7 in. Depth, 3 in.
> Light brown with dragons, and flames in white under the glaze. Mark of *Ching-hwa* period (1465). Date, 1780.

No. 727A.—Vase. Height, 12½ in. Diameter, 8 in.
> A white glaze, with branches of plum blossom, and bamboo in black under the glaze. Date, 1780.

PORCELAIN, PAINTED WITH COLOURS OVER THE GLAZE.

No. 728.—Figure of the god Fukurokujin, seated on a rock. Height, 13½ in. Width, 8 in.
> Richly decorated with floral scrolls, sprays, diapers, &c., in red and green over the glaze, and blue under it. Date, 1560.

No. 729.—Plate. Diameter, 15 in. Depth, 4 in.

    In the centre is a fabulous monster among hills and shrubs. Round the rim are bands of diaper with medallions containing floral subjects, birds, &c. Colours, red, green, and blue. This ware is known in Japan as *Gosu-aka-ye*, and is said to represent the earliest enamelled porcelain produced in China. Date, 1450.

No. 730.—Jar, with Silver rim. Height, 6½ in. Diameter, 6 in.

    Round the shoulder is a band of green with a floral scroll in red and white. The body is red, with flowers and leaves in white and green. Date, 1550.

No. 731.—Hexagonal Water Pot. Height, 7½ in. Diameter, 4 in.

    The lower portion is decorated with diapers in green and red; the upper, with diapers in red, and medallions enclosing floral subjects in red and gold. Date, 1575.

No. 732.—Water Pot, gourd shaped, the sides of the lower lobe flattened. Height, 7 in. Width, 7 in.

    On the sides of the lower lobe are large medallions with peacocks, rocks, and flowers, in red and green, blue and purple on a white ground. The rest of the surface is covered with diapers in red, relieved by flowers in white and green and large red medallions. Date, 1590. Mark, *Fu-Kwe-Kia-chi* (a valuable and beautiful vase).

No. 733.—Water Pot, with tapering neck, and long spout and handle. Height, 11 in. Width, 6 in.

    The spout, handle, base, upper portion of neck and two large heart-shaped medallions in the sides are red, with floral designs in gold. The rest of the surface has diapers in red with flowers in red and blue. Date, 1590. Mark, same as that of No. 732.

No. 734.—Vase. Height, 7 in. Diameter, 4½ in.

    Design, *Shishi* and tree peony in green, red, yellow, and blue. Date, 1600.

No. 735.—Incense Burner, hexagonal, with Lion seated on the top.

    The sides are covered with diapers in green, yellow, red, and purple. The edges are red. The lion on the top, yellow, with blue tail, green mane, and red breast. Date, 1550.

No. 736.—Incense Burner, square in section, with Lion and Ball on the top.

    The base is covered with a floral scroll in green and purple. On the sides are figure subjects in green, red, yellow, and blue. The lion is green and gold. Mark (on the rim at the top) of *Ching-hwa* period (1465). Date, 1600.

No. 737.—Incense Burner, basket-shaped. Height, 5 in. Width, 5½ in.

    The circumference is divided by bands of green diaper into panels which are perforated, except the decoration of flowers and leaves, which are solid. The top is similarly perforated. Colours, red, green, yellow and black. Date, 1659.

No. 738.—Bowl. Diameter, 6 in. Depth, 2½ in.

    Decorated inside with storks, grasses, and conventional trees in rich blue. Round the rim outside is a band of diaper in blue, and on the body are figures in red, green, and yellow enamels, separated by blue scrolls. Mark of *Kea-tsing* period (1522). Date, 1640. Black and Gold Lacquer Stand.

No. 739.—Vase. Height, 3 in. Diameter, 2½ in.

    Round the body are rudimentary characters in green and red. Round the shoulder, bands of diapers and leaves. Mark of *Ching-hwa* period (1465). Date, 1650.

No. 740.—Plate. Diameter, 11 in.

    On the face are five sages in green, blue, purple, and red. Round the rim outside are children and flowers. Mark of *Shun-ti* period (1426). Date, 1700.

No. 741.—Vase, with long neck. Height, 9 in. Diameter, 3½ in.

    Round the body are medallions containing floral subjects in green, yellow, purple, and red. The rest of the surface is covered with diapers in blue, green, yellow, and red. Date, 1700

No. 742.—Vase. Height, 14 in. Diameter, 6 in.

    Profusely decorated with figures, flowers, &c., in green, red, yellow, purple, and blue. Date, 1750.

No. 743.—Vase, square in section, with tapering base and neck. Height, 15¼ in. Side, 6 in.

    On each side is a figure, delicately executed in blue, green, red, and yellow enamels. On the shoulders are various verses of poetry, and on the neck circular medallions and half opened scrolls also containing characters. The surface of the glaze is slightly indented. Date, 1860.

No. 744.—Cups, four. Diameter, 2¾ in. Depth, 1 in.

    Decorated with rocks, flowers, cocks, hens, and chickens, in red, blue, yellow, green, and gold.

No. 745.—Incense Burner, with Black-wood Lid. Height, 2½ in.

    The body is covered with red diapers in which are characters in blue. Round the neck are two bands of blue and green diapers. Mark of *Ching-hwa* period (1465). Date, 1730.

No. 746.—Cup. Diameter, 4½ in. Depth, 2 in.

    Decoration, lotus leaves and flowers in green, blue, pink, and gold. The petals of the flowers are pierced and filled in with green glaze. Mark of *Kien-lung* period (1736). Date, 1830. Gold Lacquer Stand.

No. 747.—Cup. Diameter, 4¾ in. Depth, 2¼ in.

    Thin porcelain, with delicately executed dragons in red and blue, and round the rim a band of archaic symbols. Mark of *Ching-hwa* period (1465). Date, 1780. Black and Gold Lacquer Stand.

No. 748.—Bowl. Diameter, 6 in. Depth, 2½ in.

    Decoration, dragons, *Howo*, and flowers in green, red, blue, and yellow. Mark and date, *Kang-hi* period (1661–1722). Black and Gold Lacquer Stand.

No. 749.—Bowl. Diameter, 8 in. Depth, 3½ in.

    Decoration, on the outside, figure subjects and a band of floral scroll; on the bottom, inside, a dragon and flames. Colours, green, red, blue, and yellow. Mark of *Wan-leih* period (1573). Date, 1680. Black and Gold Lacquer Stand.

No. 750.—Bowl. Diameter, 8 in. Depth, 3½ in.

    Round the base is a double band of leaves; round the body are four large circular medallions with floral scrolls and children in blue. The space between these is filled with red diapers, &c. Mark of *Kea-tsing* period (1522). Date, 1700.

No. 751.—Bowl. Diameter, 9 in. Depth, 4 in.

    Decoration, dragons in red with clouds, flames, and a band of diaper in blue. Date, 1740.

No. 752.—Bowl. Diameter, 7 in. Depth, 3¼ in.

    Decoration, circular medallions with conventional dragons in green, blue, yellow, red, and pink. Between the medallions are flowers and leaves. Round the base is a band of diaper in green and yellow. Mark of *Ching-hwa* period (1465). Stand of carved Red Lacquer.

No. 753.—Bowl. Diameter, 7 in. Depth, 3 in.

    Round the base is a band of diaper in blue, red, and yellow. Round the body, a band of floral scroll in green, pink, and red. On the bottom, inside, is a circular scroll of leaves and flowers surrounded by a band of leaf-scroll. Mark and date, *Kien-lung* period (1736–1798).

No. 754.—Bowl. Diameter, 8 in. Depth, 4 in.

    Round the base and rim are bands of key pattern in blue. The body is covered with a wave diaper in red and white, among which are fabulous monsters in blue. Mark and date, *Kien-lung* period.

No. 755.—Bowl. Diameter, 9 in. Depth, 3½ in.

    Decoration, children at play, trees, rocks, &c., in blue, green, yellow, and red. Date, 1780.

No. 756.—Cup. Diameter, 4 in. Depth, 2½ in.

    The outside is covered with a red glaze, in which are bamboos, pines, and plums in deep blue. On the bottom, inside, are a flower and leaves. Mark, *Fu-kwe-tseng-ch'un* (wealth, honour, and long life). Date, 1680.

No. 757.—Incense Box. Diameter, 2¼ in. Depth, 1¼ in.

    Decorated with a dragon, children, floral designs, &c., delicately executed in green, blue, red, and gold. Mark of *Wan-leih* period (1573). Date, 1670.

No. 758.—Jar, with Lid. Height, 5½ in. Diameter, 3½ in.

    Light coral-red glaze with floral scrolls in gold. Mark, *Yung-po-tseng chun* (durability and long life). This piece belongs to the *Yung-lo* period (1403-1425) when ware of this design was first manufactured.

No. 759.—Bowl. Diameter, 6 in. Depth, 2¾ in.

    Decorated inside with flowers and a band of diapers in blue. The outside is covered with a coral red glaze on which are floral scrolls in gold. Mark, *Fu-kwe-kia-chi* (a valuable and beautiful vessel). Date, 1570. Black and Gold Lacquer Stand.

No. 760.—Jar, with Black-wood Lid inlaid with Silver. Height, 4 in. Diameter, 4 in.

    Covered with a coral-red glaze, in which are floral scrolls in gold. Mark of *Kea-tsing* period (1522). Date, 1680.

No. 761.—Bowl. Diameter, 6 in. Depth, 3¾ in.

    A green glaze, with purple dragons, flames and clouds. Mark and date, *Wan-leih* period (1573-1620). Black and Gold Lacquer Stand.

No. 762.—Vase, with long neck. Height, 8½ in. Diameter, 3½ in.

    Round the base and neck are bands of diaper and floral scroll in blue. On the body, dragons, clouds, and flames in green. Mark (round the neck), of *Kea-tsing* period (1522). Date, 1680.

No. 763.—Cup. Diameter, 4¾ in. Depth, 2½ in.

    A jade green glaze, on which is a floral scroll in gold. Mark, *Giok-chit-kim-hwa* (Jade body and golden flowers).

No. 764.—Bowl. Diameter, 5½ in. Depth, 2 in.

    A rich green glaze, on which are horses, flowers, clouds, flames, &c., in yellow, blue, purple, and white. Date, 1840.

(140)

No. 765.—Bowl, with Cover. Diameter, 4½ in. Height, 3½ in.

> White porcelain with a fine red crackle. Decoration, scrolls, yellow, pink, green, black, and blue, with trees, characters, &c. Date, 1840.

No. 766.—Incense Burner, square. Height, 2¾ in. Side, 1½ in.

> Decoration, a blue glaze, in which are floral scrolls, reserved. On the sides are square panels, with figure subjects and trees delicately painted in red. The inside is green. Date, 1840.

No. 767.—Bowl. Diameter, 7 in. Depth, 3¼ in.

> A rich blue *soufflé* glaze, with *Howo* and conventional designs in red and white. Mark of *Ching-hwa* period. Date, 1760. Ivory tripod Stand.

No. 768.—Bowl. Diameter, 7½ in. Depth, 3¼ in.

> A blue *soufflé* ware, decorated with trees, a man ploughing, &c., in gold. Mark and Date, *Kang-hi* period (1661-1722).

No. 769.—Vase. Height, 5½ in. Diameter, 3 in.

> Blue *soufflé* glaze, decorated with floral scrolls in gold. Date, 1780.

No. 770.—Bowl. Diameter, 7½ in. Depth, 4 in.

> A rich blue glaze with dragon, phœnixes, and conventional designs in gold. Date, 1830.

No. 771.—Plate. Diameter, 8 in.

> Blue *soufflé* ware. In the centre is an old man seated on a staff, his drapery is white and blue bordered with red. The under surface is decorated with floral sprays in blue. Mark, a leaf. Date, 1660.

No. 772.—Incense Box, in the shape of a persimmon.

> A rich blue glaze with black veins. Decoration, floral sprays in gold. On the top is a leaf of dead-leaf-coloured glaze. Date, 1800.

No. 773.—Tea Jar. Height, 3¾ in. Diameter, 2 in.

> A rich blue glaze, with floral scrolls in gold. Date, 1800.

BOCCARO WARE.

No. 774.—Tea Pot. Height, 2 in. Width, 4 in.

>Very fine dark red clay. On the lid inside are the characters *Sui peng* (water level). On the bottom, the characters *Kong-kiyok* (name of maker). Under the handle *Chi' ong ki* (seal of maker). Date, 1680.

No. 775.—Ewer, in the form of half a cocoa-nut, with pine branches and sprays in high relief. Diameter, 4 in. Depth, 2 in.

>Fine red clay. Date, 1750.

No. 776.—Ewer, in the form of a lotus leaf with curled edges. Height, 2¼ in. Length, 6 in.

>Fine white clay. On one side are two blossoms and tendrils, on the other a landcrab, in high relief. Mark, *Tin-pa tso* (made by *Tin pa*). Besides this is a line of poetry signifying:—In the autumn, seated, we watch the drooping lotus flower. Date, 1780.

No. 777.—Water vessel, square in section, with bamboo edges, spout and handle. Height, 5 in. Side, 3 in.

>On the sides are circles of bamboo with the *Swastika* inside them, in relief. Date, 1780.

KOREAN WARE.

"The records of the Emperor Sui-nin's reign (B. C. 70-29) describe an interesting event connected with Keramic industry. The peninsula now known as Korea was in that age divided into three kingdoms, called by the Chinese Sinlo, Gaoli, and Baiji; by the Japanese Shinra, or Shiragi, Kôrai or Koma, and Hiyakusai or Kudara. In the early part of Sui-nin's reign, that is to say, some sixty years before the Christian era, a prince of Shiragi, by name Ama-no-Hiboko, is said to have found his way to Japan and settled there, and Korean ware must have been known to the Japanese. Among his followers was a potter, who established a kiln in the province of Omi, and there manufactured a ware known as *Shiragi-yaki*. No authenticated specimens of this pottery are now in existence, though its production is said to have continued during many years. Neither has any account of its characteristics been transmitted, and we may fairly conclude that, whether the visit of this prince and potter from Korea be historical or not, no lasting effect was thereby produced on the Keramic art of Japan.

"Japanese antiquarians set much greater store by a subsequent event, on the truth of which, however, Western research has thrown some doubts; namely, the invasion of Korea by the Empress Jingô, about 200 A. D. True, it is not recorded in Chinese history that the Empress Jingô led this expedition, but we are told that great anarchy prevailed in the Kingdom of Wo, as Japan was then called, at the close of the second century, and that order was finally restored by a queen named Bei-mi-hoo, who was credited with the possession of magic powers. Japanese authorities assert, that after her return from Korea, the Empress Jingô fought her way to Yamato, waging fierce battles with her late husband's elder sons, and with difficulty winning the throne for her own child, and remembering that the idea of the Korean expedition is attributed to a revelation from the gods, and its success to their intervention, it is not easy to avoid the conclusion that Jingô and Bei-mi-hoo are identical, and that the conquest of Shiragi, as related in Japanese history, is confirmed by Korean annals. At all events, Japanese antiquarians maintain the truth of the story, so far as its main features are concerned, and assert that from the time of this conquest eighty ship-loads of Korean produce were sent regularly every year from Shiragi to Japan. Among the articles brought by these ships, pottery is said to have been included.

"After the days of the warlike Empress, neither tradition nor history supplies any information bearing upon Keramics, until the middle of the fifth century, when the Emperor Yûriaku ascended the throne (457 A. D.)."—From BRINKLEY's *History of Japanese Keramics*.

No. 778.—Vase, bottle-shaped. Height, 11½ in. Diameter, 6 in.

    Heavy stone-ware. A brown glaze, finely crackled, with encaustic designs in white clay. Round the shoulder are bands of diaper and vertical lines, and on the body leaves. Date, 1100.

No. 779.—Vase, with narrow base and swelling body. Height, 13 in. Diameter, 12 in.

    Stone-ware. Cream-coloured glaze finely crackled. Round the base and shoulder are lines and a band of diaper. On the sides are three large medallions bordered by broad black lines. One medallion contains the figure of an old man seated: behind him is a fir tree with a gourd hanging from its branches; before him, conventional waves and a design intended to represent the constellation of *ursa major* (*Sh'chya no hoshi*). The second medallion contains a stork flying down towards reeds and lotus plants. The third, an open lily surrounded by leaves. All the decoration is in very dark brown, and the inside is covered with a glaze of that colour. Date, 1300.

No. 780.—Vase, with narrow base and swelling body. Height, 11½ in. Diameter, 12 in.

    Stone-ware, covered inside and outside with a cream-coloured glaze. Round the neck are two bands of floral scroll in red and green enamels. Round the base, a band of conventional leaves. Round the body are three large medallions. In one is a man seated on a fish swimming in green waves: in the distance are mountains and a castle. In another are two figures, with trees, a hill, &c., in green and red. In the third, the same two figures in different positions, with flowers, trees, &c, in green and red. Date, 1300. [This is a very remarkable specimen. Korean ware decorated with coloured enamels is exceedingly rare, so much so, indeed, that its very existence has been doubted. The present specimen has been preserved in the province of Kaga since 1598.]

No. 781.—Elephant, on stand. Height, 5½ in. Length, 7 in.

    Heavy stone-ware, covered with a cream-coloured glaze slightly crackled. The trappings of the elephant are black; his feet, ears, mouth, and howdah-cloth are of a reddish brown. Date, 1260.

No. 782.—Incense Box, lozenge-shaped, with one indentation. Depth, 1 in. Diameter, $2\frac{1}{2}$ in. and $1\frac{3}{4}$ in.
> Heavy stone-ware, covered with a reddish-buff glaze. On the top is a cow in relief partially covered with a brownish green glaze. Date, 1550.

No. 783.—Water Vessel, in the shape of a man carrying a Gourd, which forms the spout. Height, 8 in. Width, 5 in.
> Stone ware, covered with a lustrous cream-coloured glaze, in which are patches of greenish brown, metallic red, and blue. Date, 1550.

No. 784.—Incense Burner, with Silver Top, square above with rounded sides. Height, $2\frac{1}{4}$ in. Width, 2 in.
> Heavy stone-ware, covered with a thin grayish glaze. On the sides are houses and rocks in relief. The legs are heads of monsters. Date, 1500.

"In addition to the beautiful ivory-white porcelain, Korea also sent to Japan, in Yoshimasa's time (1436-1480), four varieties of faience or stone-ware, of which three were essentially *rococo* in character, but the fourth, a brown *truité* pottery with inlaid designs of white clay, showed some taste and technical merit."—From BRINKLEY's *History of Japanese Keramics*.

Between the years 1596 and 1685 (the former being the date of the Japanese invasion of Korea by order of the Regent Taiko), ten Japanese Keramists visited Korea, and there produced a number of pieces, most of which were sent to Japan. The names of these potters were Oda Doki, Funahashi Genyetsu, Nakaniwa Mozo, Aoyagi Zenyemon, Nagatome Toyemon, Kokubu Risai, Matsumura Shunka, Nagano Doi, Miyagawa Doji, and Hirayama Ishun. The names of others who visited the peninsula for a similar purpose are also on record, but the times of their visits are not exactly known, being referred by some historians to a period so remote as the thirteenth century. The following numbers, from 785 to 790, are

SPECIMENS MADE BY JAPANESE KERAMISTS IN KOREA BETWEEN THE YEARS 1596 AND 1685.

No. 785.—Tripod Incense Burner, with Silver Lid. Height, 4 in. Diameter, $3\frac{1}{2}$ in.
> Stone-ware, covered with a rich green glaze, having patches of white to imitate jade. Round the body are dragons and conventional designs in relief. Round the rim and base are bands, fluting, etc. The legs are monster's heads. Date, 1650.

No. 786.—Cup, with indented rim. Diameter, 3¾ in. Depth, 3 in.

> Faience. A close-grained paste covered with a lustrous cream-coloured glaze, finely crackled. Under the glaze are storks and clouds in blue. Made by *Nakaniwa Mozo* (called also *Mosan*). Date, 1630.

No. 787.—Tripod Incense Burner, cylindrical, with Silver top. Height, 3 in. Diameter, 3 in.

> Faience. A close-grained paste covered inside and outside with a cream-coloured glaze very finely crackled. Round the body are plums, bamboos, and pines, delicately executed in light blue under the glaze. Same maker and date as No. 786.

No. 788.—Incense Burner, square in section and tapering towards the base. Height, 4½ in. Side, 3 in.

> A close-grained paste covered with a brown glaze clouded with pink and crackled. Round the rims of the body and lid are bands of key-pattern in black. On the sides are storks and clouds in white, the legs, bills, and the tips of the tails and wing feathers of the storks being black. The white portions of the designs are encaustic. Date, 1650. [*N. B.*—This is a specimen of the celebrated encaustic faience from which the Yatsushiro ware was copied.

No. 789.—Tea-Jar. Height, 2½ in. Diameter, 2½ in.

> Faience. A close-grained *pâte* covered with a reddish brown glaze flecked with cream-colour. The piece is intended to represent a bag. Round the neck is a cord in black, and in the body are lines to represent plaits. Round the waist are three conventional designs in black. Date, 1660.

No. 790.—Gourd-shaped Incense-holder. Height, 2½ in. Diameter, 2 in.

> Same clay, glaze, decoration, and date as No. 789.

KOREAN IVORY-WHITE PORCELAIN.

The specimens herein described are, by Japanese experts, unanimously attributed to Korean Keramists.

"As early as 1340 the Korean porcelain-makers were in greater repute than the Chinese. They sent across the water a ware that represents the summit of their country's Keramic achievements; an ivory-white porcelain, of beautifully fine translucent *pâte*, sometimes showing a rosy tint, and generally without any decoration other than a few engraved ideographs, flowers, or diapers. There is difficulty in distinguishing, with absolute confidence, between the ivory-white pieces attributed to Korea and those known to have been imported from China. The wares themselves do not present any differences that invite quick detection. Both alike combine properties of richness, delicacy, and restful grace which must secure for them perpetual esteem, and both would certainly be attributed to the same factories but for strong historical evidence of their distinct origin. Japanese annals are, however, emphatic on this point. They show that, about five hundred years ago, Korea began to manufacture ivory-white porcelain, and that the ware was from the first highly appreciated by the Japanese, who purchased considerable quantities of it. Without the strongest evidence to the contrary, it would be extravagant to dismiss a theory accepted so generally by native experts, supported by apparently well-authenticated specimens, and endorsed by the *Tŏ lŏ*, where we read that among the *Kŏ-li-yŏ* (wares of Korea) was a porcelain highly esteemed, ornamented with incised flowers, and resembling the *Pé-ting*, or white vases of *Ting*, which were said to have been fabricated under the Northern Sung dynasty (1004-1127). What has perplexed Western connoisseurs with regard to this ware is, that the country which is credited with its production should be the squalid, impoverished, and inartistic Korea of to-day. But, when we compare the present outcome of the Chinese kilns with their past achievements, it is easy to imagine that the artisans of Korea may have lapsed into a still deeper slough of incompetence. For, after the fifteenth century, a succession of civil wars, culminating in the Japanese invasion of 1592, completely devastated the peninsula, overthrew all evidence of its civilization, and crushed whatever germs of enterprise and progress it once possessed."—From BRINKLEY's *History of Japanese Keramics*.

No. 791.—Vase, with swelling waist and trumpet-shaped neck. Height, 9 in. Diameter, 5¼ in.

>A soft ivory-white glaze. Round the waist, leaves and tendrils are incised in the paste. Date, 1450.

No. 792.—Vase, cylindrical, with lion-head handles. Height, 6½ in. Diameter, 3 in.

> A soft ivory-white glaze with a pinkish blush. Date, 1370.

No. 793.—Stirrup Cup. Height, 4½ in. Diameter, 5 in.

> A soft ivory-white glaze with a rich pink tint. Date, 1350.

No. 794.—Cup, in the shape of a lotus flower. Height, 3 in. Diameter, 4¾ in.

> A rich ivory-white glaze with a pinkish tinge. Date, 1400.

No. 795.—Wine Cup, in the form of a convolvulus flower. Height, 2½ in. Diameter, 3½ in. and 2½ in.

> A soft ivory-white glaze with a slight pinkish tinge. On one side is a stork incised in the paste. On the other a line of poetry signifying—Let us drink ourselves to sleep, you and I. Mark, *Ten-sui* (name of maker). Date, 1400.

No. 796.—Hexagonal Box. Height, 2 in. Diameter, 3¼ in.

> Soft ivory-white glaze. On the top is a branch of the tree peony in high relief. Round this is a band of floral scroll, and on the side are plum blossoms and sprays, all in relief. Date, 1450.

No. 797.—Square Cup, tapering towards the base. Height, 2 in. Side, 3 in.

> On the sides, in sunken panels, are floral sprays, insects, a crab, and reeds, in relief. Date, 1500.

No. 798.—Water Holder, hexagonal, with swelling sides. Height, 8 in. Diameter, 6 in.

> Rich ivory-white glaze. On the top is a *shishi*. On the sides, in sunken panels, are figure subjects, trees, rocks, &c., in high relief. Date, 1500. Stand of carved Red Lacquer.

No. 799.—Vase, trumpet shaped. Height, 17½ in. Diameter, 6 in.

> Ivory-white glaze. Round the waist is a raised girdle (with four vertical ribs) covered with an incised diaper of key pattern on which are archaic designs and flowers in high relief. Above and below this belt are two horizontal grooves, and above and below these, two bands of incised leaves. Date, 1450.

No. 800.—Vase, cylindrical, with slightly tapering base and lion-head handles. Height, 13½ in. Diameter, 4½ in.

> In the paste are flowers and leaves incised, peonies on one side and lotus on the other. Date, 1450.

JUST PUBLISHED.

A CAPTIVE OF LOVE

FOUNDED UPON BAKIN'S JAPANESE ROMANCE

Kumono Tayema Ama Yo No Tsuki

(*The moon shining through a cloud-rift on a rainy night*)

BY

EDWARD GREEY

AUTHOR OF "THE GOLDEN LOTUS," "YOUNG AMERICANS IN JAPAN," "THE WONDERFUL CITY OF TOKIO," "THE BEAR-WORSHIPPERS OF YEZO," AND ONE OF THE TRANSLATORS OF THE JAPANESE HISTORICAL ROMANCE, "THE LOYAL RONINS."

Twenty-six Illustrations from the Original Work

BOSTON
LEE AND SHEPARD, PUBLISHERS
NEW YORK
CHARLES T. DILLINGHAM
1886

IN PREPARATION.

BRINKLEY'S
HISTORY OF JAPANESE KERAMICS.

BY

CAPTAIN F. BRINKLEY, R. A.,

OF YOKOHAMA.

AUTHOR OF "GOGAKU H'TORI ANNAI," "THE TIMES OF THE TAIRA," "THE TIMES OF TAIKO," &c.

This work is the result of many years research on the part of the author, who is a well-known connoisseur, and without doubt, our greatest authority upon the subject of Oriental Keramics.

It will be superbly illustrated by Kamei Shiichi, of Tôkyô, and by several of our best artists, and will be published by a well-known New York firm, who will make all further announcements concerning the book.

Lightning Source UK Ltd.
Milton Keynes UK
UKOW011813280413

209902UK00004B/119/P